Ireland Into Film

THE FIELD

D1630623

Cheryl Temple Herr

CORK **cup** UNIVERSITY PRESS

in association with
THE FILM INSTITUTE OF IRELAND

First published in 2002 by
Cork University Press
Cork
Ireland

British Library Cataloguing in Publication Data
A CIP catalogue record for this book is available from the British Library.

ISBN 1 85918 292 5

Typesetting by Red Barn Publishing, Skeagh, Skibbereen

Printed by ColourBooks Ltd, Baldoyle, Dublin

Ireland Into Film receives financial assistance from
the Arts Council / An Chomhairle Ealaíon and the Film Institute of Ireland

For David
for being there

CONTENTS

LIST OF ILLUSTRATIONS

Acknowledgements

My thanks to Jim Sheridan, Noel Pearson, Joe Dowling and Jack Conroy for agreeing to talk with me about *The Field*. Mrs John B. Keane graciously wrote to tell me that illness prevented her husband from contributing to the project. Loretto Todd helped me with Irish locutions. Niamh Nolan at Hell's Kitchen sent me material about the film, and Annemarie Naughton at Ferndale Films fielded questions. In researching the practice of 'tangling', I received much help from the librarians at the Department of Irish Folklore at University College, Dublin, the Ulster Folk Museum and the University of Ulster at Jordanstown. I was ably aided in my research by Lorry Perry and William Dolde. Dudley Andrew, R. Brandon Kershner and David Stern read the manuscript. I appreciate the time that they took from busy schedules to comment on the work; of course, all errors are my own. The series editors, Gráinne Humphreys and Keith Hopper, generously provided inspiration, information and guidance; my sincere thanks for their contribution.

The editors would also like to thank Sheila Pratschke, Lar Joye, Michael Davitt, Luke Dodd, Dennis Kennedy, Kevin Rockett, Ellen Hazelkorn, Seán Ryder, St Cross College (Oxford), Con Bushe (RTE), the School of Irish Studies Foundation and the Arts Council of Ireland.

Special thanks to Ben Cloney, Lee Murphy, Emma Keogh and the staff of the Irish Film Archive, Kate Stamworth (BFI Stills), Amelia Stein, Noel Pearson and Annemarie Naughton (Ferndale Films), Niamh Nolan (Hell's Kitchen Productions), Gus Smith and Mercier Press.

All images may be sourced at the Irish Film Centre Archive.

INTRODUCTION

The cultural text of *The Field* exists in several forms. Initially, the narrative took shape around a 1958 murder that was widely reported in the press. The story subsequently passed through the hands of two of Ireland's most popular and populist artists, John B. Keane, who composed the 1965 play, and Jim Sheridan, who wrote and directed the 1990 film. As news report, play, screenplay and film, what we call *The Field* encompasses this series of depictions, each one responding to the unsolved criminal event and, more importantly, flagging issues of its own historical moment.

The relations among these depictions are complex, and perhaps as a result there have been many critical misapprehensions of the film's relation to the Keane play. Adaptational fidelity is a perennial cinematic issue, which in this case brings into focus the purposefully oblique relation of Sheridan's work to his precursor's. In many ways, the film amounts to a critique of the play's historical and aesthetic premises. Given that the literary and cinematic texts of *The Field* present two distinct historical moments in the dismantling of traditional rural Ireland – one story composed in the 1960s, the other in the 1980s – a person who reads Keane's script (or attends a dramatic performance of *The Field*) and views the film encounters multiple intertextual messages set in shifting and sometimes contradictory social fields. How can we use these discrepancies and discontinuities to interpretative advantage?

A central argument of this study is that an emotional and intellectual appreciation of the complex transformation from play to film depends on a grasp not only of Ireland's pastoral economic history but also of issues prominent in the public discourse of the 1980s. This essay thus visits the contextual materials comprehended by the commerce of ideas between play and film as well as between

Keane's era and Sheridan's. Studying the dialogue that joins play and film, we encounter a historically situated conversation about tradition and modernity, a discussion about social change conducted both in formal monologue and in collaborative dialogue. We review the powerful ideological strictures imposed on stage and screen representations by the Irish experience of the land from the nineteenth century onwards. And we grapple not only with the forceful traditions of Irish drama but also with the assumptions prevailing in the late twentieth century about the aspirational role of an Irish national cinema and even about the nature of Irishness.

Traditional values and practices contour both the film and the play. The labour-based concern with know-how, with how things are done, and with the customs that sustain a social group forms a crucial connection between Keane's play and Sheridan's movie. In fact, Sheridan enhances this shared attention to rural practices by drawing both on his own biographical and theatrical experience and on the international cinematic tradition of representing the agricultural lifestyle under siege by social change. This essay views the characters of *The Field*, both women and men, both on stage and on screen, as repositories of cultural traditions and rural practices in transition. Taken together with their contexts and intertexts, the several versions of *The Field* briskly sketch communal experience in the Irish countryside between the mid-nineteenth-century famines and the Single European Act of 1992, which effectively changed the fundamental terms of Irish farming life.

1

KEANE AND *THE FIELD*

John B. Keane

John Brendan Keane (Plate 1) was born in Listowel in 1928 and has lived there ever since, apart from a brief exile in England (1952–54) and a short stay in Cork (1954). The story of his career as a man of public letters forms the basis of two books: Gus Smith and Des Hickey's *John B: the Real Keane* (1992) and his own pre-emptive *Self-Portrait* (1964). These works position Keane as a recorder of rural life during the fifties and sixties, an outsider to the official national theatre who ironically wrote his way both out of, and back into, the public psyche.

Keane originally wanted to become a poet, but in 1958 he turned to drama, and it is in the theatre that he has achieved his major successes. To date, in addition to nineteen published plays, he has written several novels (including his famous epistolary comedies) and many volumes of essays. Within Ireland, Keane has been arguably the most popular of the Irish playwrights working in the second half of the twentieth century. Strikingly, his work is also the least interrogated by critics. At the time of writing, the only full-length study devoted to Keane's drama is Sister Marie Hubert Kealey's *Kerry Playwright: Sense of Place in the Plays of John B. Keane* (1992). Anthony Roche's *Contemporary Irish Drama* (1995) provides one explanation for this critical neglect by associating Brian Friel, Tom Murphy and Thomas Kilroy with the *haute couture* of Beckett while excluding Keane (along with Hugh Leonard) on the grounds that the two 'benefit from a different critical orientation to show their dramatic qualities'.[1] Keane has often been handled in print with this kind of understated obliquity, presumably to avoid a harsher and perhaps more begrudging evaluation of his extraordinary popularity.

Plate 1. John B. Keane.

Much of Keane's theatrical energy emerges from the popular melodrama tradition of the mid nineteenth century and early twentieth century.[2] The plays of J. W. Whitbread, P. J. Bourke and Dion Boucicault did not resemble the austere folk drama favoured by the Abbey Theatre. Keane's early, persistent rejection by Ireland's premier company signals the extent to which he embraced the grotesqueries of native melodrama while simultaneously pursuing a dramatic mode that might be called tendentious realism. It has been all too easy for critics of Keane's work to foreground only a single aspect of his writing and on that partial basis to pronounce its limitations. Keane has been taken to task for being too popular or too uncouth, too inflammatory or too evasive. Efforts to label his work – whether in the peasant tradition, the melodramatic mode, or even the zone of fabulous extravagance – have demonstrated how slippery and labile Keane's writing, at its best, can be, and how wide a performance palette he offers to directors. For much of his career, this mixture of modes guaranteed that Keane would offend many metropolitan viewers and that his serious work would be persistently misread as trivial and thus excludable from dramatic history.

Indeed, Keane has written about being dismissed by critics, misrepresented by journalists and attacked by anonymous letter-writers. In response, he emphasizes the honesty that one needs in order to be a writer, the writer's ability 'to convey the great joys, the great sorrows, the great madnesses and the great hurts in himself and others'.[3] For Keane, emotional truths cannot be plumbed according to the dictates of a single, fashionable style. And his work gained popularity despite performances that Keane has described as 'shoddy' and played for laughs.[4] Keane's suspension between popular acclaim and recurrent critical ridicule persisted for almost thirty years. As the passage of time has shown, the writing also yields to more profound staging. By the eighties, the complex force of Keane's writings gradually won out over stereotyped views of his plays. By exploring rural customs under challenge, Keane approached the great emotions of which he speaks. Work that was launched in local productions by the unsubsidized theatre and that emphasized the regional specificity of Keane's best writing has become, in a Europe of the Regions, a sign of his prescience and contemporaneity.

Nevertheless, the serious, routine acceptance of Keane by the national theatre did not occur until a Keane revival took place under the aegis of Ben Barnes and Joe Dowling, the latter then the artistic director at the Abbey. In an essay cheerily announcing 'John B. Keane: Respectability at Last!', Anthony Roche calls Keane the 'longest excluded' from the national theatre of those playwrights who began writing in the 1950s, and he agrees that by 1989 Keane had been recognized by the national theatre as 'a major playwright'. The plays most often receiving praise constitute a *de facto* trilogy. They are *Sive* (originally produced in 1959 and staged by the Abbey in 1985), *The Field* (first produced in 1965 and mounted by the Abbey in 1987) and *Big Maggie* (first performed in 1969 and presented on the Abbey stage in 1988).

From the outset, Keane's predilection for the comic quip unsettled his claim to high-cultural acceptance but effortlessly promoted his general popularity. Regularly holding forth on RTÉ's *Late Late Show*, Keane took on the mantle of witty, candid raconteur while not entirely eschewing the cloak of stage Kerryman. This persona made frequent appearances in newspaper interviews, Irish radio and television shows, and after-dinner speeches.

Keane's comic writing has extended in many directions. His 1989 collection, *The Power of the Word*, consists of some five hundred witticisms culled from Keane's writings, speeches and interviews. Many of these sayings fit the classic form of the Irish bull. For example, in *The Field*, the Bull lives up to his name when he bitterly observes, 'The likes of us that's ignorant has to be clever.' They also include other forms of paradoxical wit, as in 'Spirit of Kerry', an essay written for Ryanair, in which Keane opines, 'There is no such thing as a conventional Kerryman. If you try to analyse him he changes his pace in order to generate confusion.'[5] As such witticisms glide by the reader, they evoke a tantalizing series of scenes, the germs of dramas both extant and notional, both lighthearted and poignant.

So beloved has Keane been as writer and citizen that in 1979 Mercier Press published a tribute volume called *Fifty Years Young*. He has also received many awards, among which are membership of Aosdána (the Irish Academy of Arts), life membership of the Royal Dublin Society, the *Sunday Tribune* Award for Literature, and honorary doctorates from Trinity College, Dublin, (which holds Keane's manuscripts) and Marymount College, New York. Completing his certification as a major presence in twentieth-century Irish letters, in 1998 Keane received the coveted Gradam medal from the National Theatre Society for exceptional contributions to Irish theatre. Emer O'Kelly, covering the prestigious award for the *Sunday Independent*, suggested that 'the original unwillingness to accept Keane's uncompromising view of rural Ireland had something to do with its truth; for a generation just removed from the primal cruelty of the small farm, he was an uncomfortable reminder of roots barely below the surface'. The hedging tones in which he has been praised speak volumes about the reluctance of urban Ireland to acknowledge kinship with Keane's mountainy folk. O'Kelly observed that 'we've finally begun to confront the demons Keane so graphically depicts'.[6]

Certainly, the issues that punctuate Keane's works – greed and jealousy, resentment and domestic abuse, pagan attachments and harsh authoritarianism, verbal indulgence and sexual repression – have emerged from the social shadows and are a regular part of public discourse in twenty-first-century Ireland. For his part, Keane has never been shy about witnessing to the inner demons that have congenitally tormented him. A recent interview confirms that an 'innate turbulence' remains with him even in his elder years.[7] Perhaps for this reason, Keane has always been highly critical of religious authority, especially when it loses touch with everyday life and consensual morality. He has routinely decried social injustice, ideological coercion, and the refusal of pleasure. But these topics do not exhaust the existential anxiety to which Keane personally and theatrically attests. To quiet his fundamental spiritual and emotional turbulence, Keane has often withdrawn 'to a wild place for days at a time' where, Suibhne-like, he has found comfort in unruly nature.[8]

At the same time that he has craved merger with the sublime, he is a staunch anti-romantic, committed to unveiling the truths behind the stereotypes that Ireland has often been caught up in and hence traded upon. That said, it is worth repeating that the realism that Keane's fictions press on the reader is never free from grotesquerie, melodrama, ironic self-commentary and satire. Brinsley MacNamara, a writer with whom Keane shares a caustic edge, speaks of 'the traditional Gaelic dread of satire', from which only the local satirist was free.[9] It may seem remote at this date to claim a connection between the ancient bard composing community-exposing satire and the biting rural realism that achieves an uneasy dominance in Keane's writing. Nevertheless, assuming the position of genial storyteller with a lethal double-edge to his discourse, Keane has undoubtedly occupied a highly traditional social role, all the while deflecting attention from the more sinister of his pronouncements through the defence mechanisms of witty observation and gentle appreciation of his home county. Keane has applied a comic salve to the hurts he has probed, but he has also ruthlessly exposed social and familial dysfunction.

The apparent contradictions of Keane's compositional legacy eloquently attest to the social contradictions seen in Ireland between 1928 and the millennium. The moments that he depicts best are transitional moments, when a locale must react to new demands on its cultural and economic resources, when a ritual comes under the stress of social disruption. In these situations, questions of marriage and property allocation rush forward, as do a host of ethical considerations and emotional extravagances in which Keane always revels.

Keane's *The Field*

The Field is Keane's best-known work, both in Ireland and internationally. First produced by the Olympia in 1965, the play was revived in 1987 and taken by the Abbey the following year to Moscow and Leningrad at the request of the USSR Ministry of Culture and Government, members of which had seen the production in Dublin. Edited by Ben Barnes to eliminate narrative repetition, the revised text of *The Field* was published by Mercier Press in 1991.

The play relates the story of the Bull McCabe, a small farmer who rents a four-acre pasture from a local widow, Maggie Butler. When the widow puts the field up for auction, the Bull arranges with the auctioneer and local publican, Mick Flanagan, to fix the sale. However, word of the auction gets out to a Galway native transplanted to England, a man named William Dee, who travels to the town of Carraigthomond to buy the land with the aim of building a factory on the site. While trying to intimidate Dee into leaving town, McCabe and his son Tadhg accidentally murder him. Out of fear and custom, the town closes ranks behind McCabe. The publican's son, Leamy, wants to respond to the impassioned call of the church and the law for information about Dee's murderer, but his mother begs him to remain silent rather than put himself and his family in danger.

This drama falls into two acts, each with three scenes. Of those six scenes, all but one take place inside Mick Flanagan's pub. The exception has been recognized by theatrical scholars as one of the most powerful scenes in Irish theatre – where, in deep night, the Bull and Tadhg wait for William Dee while comfortably eating sandwiches and chatting. Father and son discuss why the Bull and his wife have not spoken for the last eighteen years; the Bull reveals that he once killed a tinker's[10] pony caught grazing in his field, and it was on the basis of this affront, exacerbated by the Bull's physical abuse of her, that Mrs McCabe refused to speak to or have sex with her husband again. The Bull and Tadhg hear a jet plane in the distance and mention the indoor bathroom and electric light that the Bull has installed to curry favour with his wife. In contrast to these signs of modernity is Tadhg's eager revelation that he has his eye on a local girl who, according to tradition, would come to a marriage with acreage in tow. From such harmless chitchat in the shadows, the two emerge to frighten and ultimately kill William Dee. The play is full of such verbal gracenotes and startling contrasts, but the structure is spare. *The Field* concentrates on the choice between authoritarian morality and local folkways, between the rules of administered society and what in the film the Bull calls 'the law of the land'.

But what, precisely, is at stake in this contrast of legalities? To answer this question, we first need to meditate on the place of the small farmer within his community and the social regulations that must be observed in Carraigthomond. We might begin by noting how the farmer McCabe is known by his peers. Does McCabe's nickname signal his overbearing nature, his identification with the agricultural economy, or both? A lot depends on who is speaking to the Bull and in what situation his name is invoked. Keane addresses this social decorum in a short essay entitled 'Kerry Nick-Names'.[11] He shows that even seemingly 'belittling' nicknames often refer not only to personal traits but also to the victories of one's ancestors and thus to an individual's place in local history and the social hierarchy. In the very first scene of Keane's play, a character known as Bird O'Donnell greets McCabe with a cheery, 'How's the Bull?' and receives a petulant rebuke: 'Who gave you the right to call me Bull, you pratey-snappin' son-of-a-bitch.'[12] This exchange between the Bird and the Bull, set against Keane's explanation of nicknaming in Kerry, points to the delicate balance that McCabe must preserve between familiarity and status-maintenance. P. W. Joyce reminds us that the standard of value in Celtic culture from prehistory onwards was always cattle: 'the old word for a cowherd was *bóchaill* or *buachaill* [boohil]; from *bo*, a cow'.[13] The Bull's status and his name are one. In a culture of animal breeders, he is overtly identified with kin and kine, and he cannot allow the value of his sobriquet to be reduced to that of the Bird's.

Patrick Wallace, director of the National Museum of Ireland, underscores the literal currency of the Bull's title: 'The key to the understanding of Ireland – Irish history, Irish archaeology, Irish culture, the great sagas – [is that] everything is based on cattle. Cows are everything and everywhere.'[14] Through his nickname, the Bull allows and even embraces the collective identification of himself and his family with their cattle and, by extension, with the land on which they graze and drop manure. They are all part of a single calculus of rural life that encompasses the specific pastoral economy of the Bull's townland and the traditional economy of the nation. As Estyn Evans points out, ancient Irish territorialism was based on the needs of livestock.[15] This fact underlies sectarian violence and the motivation for several versions of nationalism. Keane emphasizes that the Bull as cattle breeder cannot be separated from the Bull as landowner and the Bull as murderer. As Keane presents him and as Ray McAnally, Niall Tóibín and Joe Lynch have famously depicted McCabe onstage, the Bull remains an undaunted spokesperson for indigenous attitudes sanctioned by history if not by administered culture. Beyond their value in explaining the Bull's character, his obsession with the land, his ferocity in its defence and even the public use of his nickname signify these historical continuities, as well as the delicate ecology of the traditional socius.

Within this local system, the determination of who should own the widow's field does not rest solely on sentiment or even on custom. It involves the history of land reform legislation in the British Isles. In his enlightening book *States of Mind* (1983), Oliver MacDonagh reviews this legislation in the chapter on 'Property'. He isolates two intersecting but incongruent conceptions of property prevailing in Ireland:

> The term 'property', as loosely used in nineteenth-century Ireland, carried a double meaning. But the dualism was not immediately apparent. This was so because one version was clearly articulated and expressed precisely in legislation, whereas the other was only to be inferred from agrarian conduct and the coarse clichés of a peasantry.[16]

After the 1801 Act of Union, Irish land was regulated legally by English notions of property. However, from the 1840s onwards, while Ireland was rocked by famine and agrarian agitation, a *laissez-faire* landlordism was gradually replaced by legislated reforms, specifically by contractual regulation of the landlord–tenant relationship and the incremental purchase of the land by peasant farmers.

On the other hand, 'Landed relationships in Ireland were often too intricate' to be governed entirely by such laws. The 'peasant's view of property' rested on a communal view of land ownership, albeit a much qualified one.[17] MacDonagh does not invoke the Irish word *ceantair* (meaning 'region'), but it is surely important to note that in the Irish-language logic marked by this word a group not only owned the land on which it dwelled but was viewed as inseparable from its native territory. The 'subterranean challenge to the formally dominant theory of property' relied on this notionally indissoluble identity with the land. It thus underlay the emergence of the eighteenth-century Whiteboys and other rural secret societies, with their sense of a 'rival legal code and machinery of enforcement'.[18]

By the 1850s, constitutional agitation for fixity of tenure, free sale and fair rent attempted to bring native concepts of land ownership into legislative language. MacDonagh elaborates on 'fixity of tenure', the contested principle most relevant to the Bull's case:

> The first of the three objectives in the programme of the Tenant League, fixity of tenure, seemed in flat contradiction to the received idea of property in Britain. How could a tenant have a 'right' to occupancy if he did not fulfil the conditions of the contract which had placed him on his holding? But the Irish tenant was pursuing a line of reasoning which never intersected the atomistic-contractual. It was perfectly true that the claim to fixity of tenure implied a 'right' to occupancy. But the context of such a claim in Ireland was a world apart from that used in parliamentary debates. By fixity of tenure the Irish peasant meant that the tenant could not be removed because he was inefficient, or undeferential, or disgruntled, or a Catholic, or defiant in voting against his landlord's direction. None of these was regarded as a proper reason for uprooting a man and his family from the soil in which, Anteus[sic]-like, they had 'grown' and 'grew'.[19]

The Bull fully embodies these indigenous ideas. His name, his status in the community and his inability to imagine or accommodate social change all manifest the phenomenological continuity customarily attributed to life in rural Ireland. The Bull does not do homage to the law of the state, however many reforms it had gone through by the date of Keane's play. Rather, in learning from his father how to tend the land, the Bull absorbed the attitudes underpinning that form of care and became inseparable from the field and its implied freight of traditional mores.

Maggie Butler certainly understands this situation. She knows that two forms of law coexist uneasily in the community. To establish her position in the tacit debate, she tells Mick Flanagan in scrupulous detail that the land was 'willed to me by my husband five years ago. 'Twas purchased under the Land Act by my husband's father, Patsy Butler. He willed it to my husband and my husband willed it to me. I'm the registered owner of the field' (Keane, p. 11). However, her liminal social status undermines her claim. A widow without a child, she has no one to make use of the land. A woman apparently without extended family, she has no one to defend her rights. Roughly of the Bull's class, she is also in the anomalous position of being the Bull's landlord. All in all, she can readily be excluded from the tacit workings of the local system and community relations, which conspire towards the view that selling the field to anyone but McCabe is, according to the 'law of the land', unjust.

MacDonagh helps us to understand the notion of free sale in a way that further unpacks this dilemma. Free sale, he notes, 'undoubtedly implied a degree of co-possession between the lessor and lessee'. Thus, the renter

> believed it to be but 'natural' that he should transmit – or at least be enabled to transmit – his holding to his heirs in the same fashion as the proprietor would pass down his demesne to his successors. The tenant also saw himself as mingling his labour with the earth which was temporarily in his charge, and thereby establishing a saleable interest by his very tenure. If therefore he were removed or wished to leave, he felt that his investment of time and effort should be rewarded.

It was Gladstone's Land Act of 1870 that recognized a tenant's right to be compensated for improving what he rented. By 1881, the Land Act formally underwrote the idea of landlord–tenant joint ownership, an inherently 'unstable condition'.[20]

Legislation after the 1880s favoured tenant ownership. Keane's play is set in 1965. A peasant proprietor of the contested field in all but name, the Bull cannot accept Maggie's right to sell off her property without consulting him. There is no doubt that the Bull has added value to the field that he can never recover if she sells to another party. MacDonagh admits that the price of land depended not only on the open market but also on the will of the immediate community: 'The values set upon land and buildings were in the last analysis the social values of the Irish countryside, the traditional estimates of right relations between owner, occupier and worker, and of their familial needs.'[21] This will was expressed, when all else failed, through what were called agrarian 'outrages'. The Bull McCabe is nothing if not Irish in his conception of land usage and the land–tiller relation. His violent reactions, which may strike a contemporary audience – especially one that is urban and non-Irish – as grotesquely melodramatic, claim legitimacy in this ancient vision of property. As Keane frames the story, the Bull represents a holistic way of life struggling for survival.

In Parnell's time, many of the clergy were sympathetic to the tenant-farmers, but in Keane's work the clergy in power tend to be self-serving outsiders who are out of touch with the remaining traces of the elder faiths and practices that sustain social cohesion. Throughout his fictions, Keane attacks the complicity of the Church with a constricting and destructive 'solution' to Irish postcolonial economic woes – the forced emigration of the young. In all of Keane's work except for the most throwaway comic writings, there is a pointed critique of the clergy. So it is that, after the Bull has purchased the field, he says to Father Murphy:

When you'll be gone, Father, to be a Canon somewhere and the Sergeant gets a wallet of notes and is going to be a Superintendant, Tadhg's children will be milking cows and keeping donkeys away from our ditches. That's what we have to think about and if there's no grass, that's the end of me and mine. (Keane, p. 80)

In the Bull's eyes, churchways are indistinguishable from stateways. And a public auction of land is merely the contemporary, government-sanctioned form of the older curse of eviction and exile.

The Tangler

Despite the difference in status between the Bull and the Bird, McCabe receives substantial help from his cohort when he bids for the widow's property, and it is the Bird who memorably opens the play. The first scene establishes the constant, collective micro-management of a social field where much information is tacit, individual status is closely guarded and explanations often remain oblique. Scene 1 emphasizes not only the communal struggle to negotiate conflicting conceptions of property and legality but also the outright gamesmanship governing the sale of the field. These topics are entered upon lightly but immediately when the curtain rises on the young Leamy Flanagan 'playing pitch and toss' with his siblings. Coming upon this innocent gaming, the Bird humorously refers to Carraigthomond as 'like Las Vegas with all the gambling going on' (Keane, p. 7). Wise for his years, Leamy responds with a knowing barb, 'How's trade?' This exchange suggests that playing games, doing business and simply chatting engage the same skills of strategizing and one-upmanship – a proposition amply confirmed by the rest of Scene 1.

When Mick the publican enters his place of business, he sends his children offstage to their dinner, chides the Bird for his habitual whistling and, when the Bird surprisingly pays for his drink rather than begging for credit, pointedly asks, 'Who did you take down now?'

> BIRD: Take down! That's illegal, that is! I could get you put in jail for that. A pity I hadn't a witness. 'Twould pay me better than calf-buying.[22]
> MICK: There must be great money in calf-buying.
> BIRD: Not as much as there is in auctioneering.
> MICK: Very funny! Very funny! Don't forget I have to use my head all the time.
> BIRD: Not half as much as I do. Did you ever try to take down a small farmer?[23]

For many contemporary readers, especially those who are not Irish, this interchange has an elliptical, puzzling quality. We need to be explicit about how the term 'take down' conveys the gaming aspect of the local economy and, within Keane's microcosm, suggests the prevalence of such strategizing throughout Irish culture.

Keane's 1991 novel, *Durango*, helps to clarify this opening strophe of *The Field*. It seems likely that the story Keane tells in this novel underlay his initial depiction of the Bird many years earlier. *Durango* is set just before World War II in the environs of Tubberlick, a village with a quarterly cattle and pig fair. Although prices are expected to rise during wartime, when demand is high, the prices that Mark Doran sees at the market are 'inexplicably low', regardless of the quality and age of the livestock:

> Mark Doran had long suspected the visiting buyers of being part of a ring and his suspicions were reinforced by the fact that cattle prices in Tubberlick were always a fraction behind those in other villages of the countryside. The trouble was that the villages in question were too far distant, the nearest ten and the furthest fifteen miles . . . 'Cattle jobbers have to live too,' his mother would say whenever he voiced his

dissatisfaction after a frustrating day of haggling at the quarterly fair.[24]

Like other small farmers, Doran lives off marginal increases in market prices. He wants to gather information from other farmers about the deals that they strike, but he faces the 'cloak of secrecy which his neighbours insisted in drawing over cattle prices . . . He knew the shame and degradation he himself had experienced when he was forced to sell cattle at less than their value.' To save face, farmers did not talk of such things: 'buying and selling were conducted in confessional whispers. At the end of the day there was no means by which one could arrive at an average price.'[25]

This customary obfuscation enabled price-fixing, and Keane associates this sort of illegality with the Bird O'Donnell in the opening scene of *The Field*. Such activity seems to take place most often in pubs, at least in Keane's world. In *Durango*, it is the local publican who pays the cattle jobbers (low-level traders) to fix prices. Confronted with an accusation to this effect and echoing *The Field*, the pubkeeper says, 'There's witnesses here . . . and if you make any more accusations against me you'll answer in a court of law.'[26]

Durango provides further background to the Bird's likely activities in the community. Having formed a small consortium of his cattle-selling neighbours, Mark Doran takes the lot to far-off Trallock town for sale. Speaking of Trallock fair, the narrator talks about:

> local knackers whose true vocations lay not in locating under-priced cattle but rather in identifying backwards and uninformed rustics who could be panicked into selling in a hurry if the knacker was proficient at his job. Only that morning a knacker had complained to Flannery that he would require an extra commission as his immortal soul was in danger of damnation. Intrigued, Jacko Flannery asked for details.

'The last time I was in confession,' the knacker lamented, 'the priest told me he could not give me absolution over I taking down small farmers all the time.'[27]

Judging from this discussion, we can infer that the Bird has been associated with price-fixing – or at least is fair game for Mick's jocular jibes in this direction.

In short, the Bird fills the traditional role of go-between or facilitator, and the opening scene indicates as much in language that emphasizes the web of family, tradition and commercial ritual that the Bull will rely on to fight the widow. The Bird facilitates McCabe's cause by making false bids against the Bull during the auction (Plate 2), helping to ensure that the niceties are observed despite the attempted price-fixing.

There are indigenous terms for what the Bird does by way of making a living: he is a 'tangler' or 'blocker'. A 1932 government report speaks of blockers as:

> persons who attend local fairs and use their skill in spotting animals suitable for the trade of large dealers and shippers. They immediately start bargaining with the seller, and so prevent a legitimate dealer getting the opportunity of opening a deal. This state of affairs goes on until a dealer comes along who is prepared to give a few shillings to 'get in on the cattle'.[28]

Genealogical research from the late nineteenth and early twentieth centuries shows that many unlanded rural workers in Ireland and England described themselves as cattle or pig jobbers, all of whom, including tanglers, drovers, dealers, blockers and sundry hangers-on, frequented markets with the aim of extracting their twopence-worth from the rituals of trading. It is this world of semi-intrigue and cunning that Keane locates at the heart of the townland's most important transactions.

Plate 2. The auction.

These activities, second nature in Keane's countryside but relatively invisible from the urban exterior, have mostly remained in the shadows of Irish representation. In *Michael Joe: a Novel of Irish Life* (1965), William C. Murray establishes himself as one of the few twentieth-century writers explicitly to describe tangling and enlarges upon the portrait that Keane provides in *Durango*. He does so as he presents shopkeeper Michael Joe's efforts to get into the cattle business:

> At the fair there was nothing but men bargaining over cattle, pitting wits against wits in a struggle for top penny in the market place. Any trick, any strategem was fair. Any means of blinding a buyer could be employed. The seller tried to hide faults, the buyer to find them. Michael Joe knew this.

He was unsure. But the compulsion to enter the primitive world where he was thrown on his own resources, to rise or fall, was too much for him.[29]

Murray lavishes many details on Michael Joe's experiences at fair-going. His initial success at the hand-slapping rituals of purchase is followed by his absorption into acting as a blocker for others' bargaining, revelling in the dynamism of the marketplace:

> There was a sense of purpose and goal in even the slightest approach or greeting. When a man walked up to you you did not know what he had on his mind. He might let you know in a roundabout way that there was a milch cow somewhere in the fair he was interested in. Would you vet for him? Or make a bid, a false bid, to find out what the fellow wanted for her. Feints, darts and dodges. Name calling.[30]

The fierce competition, a vicious and taunting quality within that struggle, emerges in Murray's knowing prose. The morality of the situation exists elsewhere than in the territory patrolled by gardaí and clergy – a territory embedded in tradition and embodied in the tanglers' motions and patter. A certain amount of harassment, of purchase on another's intentions, entered into these mediations. Hence, the bargaining over land that Keane shows us falls into the pattern of expectations and ruses which can easily go badly wrong.

It is certainly in this context that we must view former Abbey Theatre artistic director Joe Dowling's comment that the Bird occupies a crucial position in *The Field*. In Dowling's view, the best embodiment to date of the Bird on stage has been Keane's brother Eamon, a comedian who allowed the Bird to emerge as the playwright's self-projection into the drama – the one who sees what is going on and remains at a distance, not caught up in the dire events onstage.[31] Thus the Bird is, like John B. Keane in his real-life role as both publican and writer, an observer of local life. The Bird is also not above strategic, creative meddling. He is very much a figure from British versions of the stage Irishman by way of Boucicault, Synge and O'Casey – the local *shaughraun* (trickster), at once gormless and acute. Although the Bird may also be categorized as a jester figure in the Greco-Shakespearean tradition, playing Fool to the Bull's Lear, his designation as 'tangler' provides the central metaphor of Keane's play.

Among other things, the Bird's tangling extends to his being both gofer and go-between. He fulfils an active role in the social structure, culling information and weaving alliances. Keane's work as a whole suggests that traditional society has reserved a place for the individual who carries information and parlays transactions into ever-more-slippery exchanges. Keane specifically reminds us of this function in *Durango* when we are told that calf-dealers 'brought news from faraway places as well as more intimate and often sensational disclosures from the less forthcoming of her immediate neighbours. Such revelations, false or true, had considerable trade value at mealtimes and even during sale negotiations.'[32]

Keane's opening scene puts the Bird in conversation with the publican to display these generative mediating activities. There to be made use of, the Bird is always cadging for his kickback. Viewed in local terms, tangling involved nothing underhand. People expected this nonconfrontational style of confrontation from a convenient third party working to deflect stand-offs and showdowns in a society caught between conflicting views of property and justice. The Bird's bargain with the Bull is the originary contradiction that the play builds on, even though most of the characterizing behaviour remains implicit in the dialogue.

Immediately following the 'take down' exchange which sets the terms for the ensuing conflict, Maggie Butler enters the pub to put up her field for auction, and the main action of the play gets under way. The Bird is known to Maggie only by sight, so he has little part in the exchange between Mick and Maggie. However, when she exits, the Bird observes, 'You've a nice tricky job facing you now' (Keane,

p. 13). The Bird instantly sees beyond Mick's 'business is business' stance towards the actuality of trade negotiations in the close-knit rural community.

The Bird's trademark manipulative skill emerges when Mick goes for his dinner and his wife Maimie takes over the pubkeeping. The Bird, now out of money, asks for his third half-whiskey. When Maimie asks, 'Have you the price of it?' the Bird counters, 'No . . . but I'm selling two calves this evening.' Her businesslike refusal, 'Cash on the line only,' prompts the Bird's observation, 'By God, you're an amazin' woman the way you keep your appearance. I mean, after nine children, you're still the best-lookin' bird in Carraig-thomond.' Identifying his nickname with her putative youthfulness, the Bird wins over her scepticism when he attributes his observation to the solicitor's son, and she acknowledges, 'I'm not bad when I'm dressed up . . . if I had the time, that is.' At which point the Bird is given his half-whiskey, and Maimie has purchased a captive audience for her denunciation of the begrudgers of the town, those 'sanctimonious bitches on the way to the altar of God every Sunday with their tongues out like bloody vipers for the body of Christ, and the host is hardly melted in their mouths when they're cuttin' the piss out of one another again!' (Keane, pp. 14–15).

While the conversation continues, Maimie is typing the notice for the auction, and she struggles to read Mick's writing. In reference to the field's 'access to the river', she asks the Bird how to spell 'access'. His reply, 'A...X...I...S', malaproptically indicates his central position in the entanglements to follow, when in comes the Bull. Without the customary salutation, the Bull asks about Maggie Butler. To buy information, he offers the Bird a drink. Rather than the half-whiskey that the Bird requests, however, the Bull orders him a cheaper bottle of stout and proceeds to pump him for details about the widow's intentions. Every stage of the conversation is negotiated, every drink purchased with knowledge. The Bull plants his own information by telling the Bird the amount he is willing to pay for the field and by reminding him that 'Half this village is related to me and them that isn't is related to my wife' (Keane, p. 18), a situation ensuring that the Bull will be the only local bidder for the property.

Attempting to extricate himself from what looks like a no-win bargaining situation, the Bird indicates that his wife will be keeping dinner waiting for him, a claim that McCabe rejects. He intimidates the Bird into staying, and he shouts for the auctioneer. The Bull also speaks to his son with 'genuine affection' while they assert their 'rights' to the field. Again the Bird tries to 'slip away' and again is forced to remain, the Bull using nick-nomenclature to undermine the Bird's status: 'Can't you sit still? 'Tis no wonder they call you after a bird. You're worse than a bloody sparrow!' (Keane, p. 20). The Bull insists on a private conversation with Mick, and Mick buys Maimie's departure with money for the hairdresser. Asserting his claim, one purchased with both 'hard-earned' rent and manure, the Bull tells the intimidating story of how he and Tadhg trapped and killed a donkey that was eating their grass. The storytelling is beautifully orchestrated between father and son in yet another display of folkways that sustain social cohesion.

From the outset, the Bull is intent on engineering the auction to his advantage. He persuades Mick neither to notify the papers nor to post bills for the auction; he speculates that one of his grand-uncles could 'be dying that day' and require Maggie's solicitor to be writing his will at the time of the auction. Claims of illegality are laughed away by the Bull, who also agrees to pay the bribe that Mick craftily demands for his services. The Bird is called upon to add his voice to the transaction. Witnessing with 'solemn oath' that the Bull pays Mick a deposit of £20, the Bird has become integral to the transaction and is himself paid a small sum and a final half-whiskey.

This negotiation has not been easy. The Bull is described as showing 'an ecstasy of accomplishment' (Keane, p. 26). He has demonstrated his practical know-how in a virtuoso feat of economic and social competence. Relieved of worry, he rhapsodizes over the plantings that his labour has encouraged in the widow's field. He crows about his ability to foresee that the widow needed money – all indicating the keen observational skills needed to keep track of such rural dealings and to triumph not over them but within them.

Never able to rest, the Bull quickly needs to deflect another danger. The Sergeant enters the pub to question him about the death of a donkey, and the Bull calls on the Bird to testify that they were playing cards at the time that the donkey was heard crying out while being beaten. All of which allows the Bull to end the scene with a big finish: '. . . a Sergeant might get his face split open one night and all the guards in Ireland wouldn't find out who did it . . . not if they searched till Kingdom Come!' (Keane, p. 29).

This long first scene occupies fully a third of the play's text, all of it composed of cadging, angling, bargaining and coercing – ringing changes in the interstices of the tightly linked social system. For anyone anticipating a romanticized view of rural life, this scene flagrantly undermines that expectation. It does so, however, by drawing elliptically on transactional rituals characteristic of that life. Beyond the land, and just as important in stabilizing the social group, is the story of markets, fairs and bargaining practices on which this scene liberally draws.

Whether a tangler was merely disreputable or also entertaining, he was integral to the texture of Irish rural life. Having lived outside his native Galway for over a decade, William Dee has acclimatized to English ways and bafflingly fails to take seriously the local rituals that are to become his undoing. And as a *de facto* Briton, he would never be able to buy his way into the Irish community or even to co-opt the Bird's services in a situation that would leave the tangler without protection from the Bull and his extended family. Rather, the utter hopelessness of Dee's efforts and the superficial hold of legal discourse on tacit folkways conspire to make much of the actual drama happen elsewhere than in the auction confrontation. In this case, the machinery of possession, defence and revenge is far too complex for a lone interloper to challenge successfully or for a cadre of tanglers to manage.

Local History

The story that Keane tells is based on an actual murder that took place in the townland of Reamore in the Stacks Mountains. As the newspapers reported it, Maurice Moore and Dan Foley fell out over the siting of a boundary ditch and, in November of 1958, Moore was found strangled to death. Foley always protested his innocence, and he was never formally charged with the crime, though many in Kerry believed him to be guilty. During schoolboy summers in the Stacks Mountains in the late twenties and early thirties,[33] Keane accrued an intimate knowledge of the people that he met there. Anthony Roche reports that Keane 'knew both the man who was killed and the man who committed the murder'. Keane told Roche, 'I went to see the man who committed the murder and he saw me, because I was one of them. I had really been reared up there.'[34] In Keane's view, Foley suffered terribly in his isolation after the murder of his neighbour, and the play demonstrates Keane's sympathy for and understanding of this individual. The play attempts to excavate his motivation, to demonstrate the pressures that might have issued in just such a real-life melodrama.

It is clear that the murder came to represent, not only for Keane but also for the nation, a moment of breakdown in rural mores precipitated in part by the pressures of modernization. Of the time spent in Renagown, Keane has said, 'What was happening there at the time was that a way of life was changing, *not* from rural to urban, but a change within the rural community itself. And I was witness to that change.' He adds that these people, using the new technology for turfcutting, 'dragged themselves out of the past and into the present, I fear rather too hastily . . .'.[35] His early experience acquainted him intimately with the struggle to maintain or revise rural farmways and the frequent economic necessity of emigration, which was prompted by the state's failure to provide employment based in a stable economy and traditional roles.

In Keane's play, Bull McCabe insists on his innocence, defies the authorities, coerces his neighbours and stands firm for his right to the land that he had rented and improved. He and his son are not cowed by the dramatized events, and we see them holding onto their way of life despite the massive social changes and economic devastation that characterized rural Ireland in the 1950s. Even though the action is cast in 1965, the Bull – whether ferociously as in the McAnally production (Plate 3) or more quietly as in later takes on the role – resists the changes that have become inevitable. In this sense, the Bull is less an individual than a representative patriarch, whose sensibility speaks of adherence to deep, changeless traditions.

The time during which Keane lived in Renagown is close to the period in which Conrad Arensberg did his initial ethnographic fieldwork in County Clare towards his groundbreaking study *The Irish Countryman* (1937). The 'familist' system that Arensberg described is well-known and has been summarized in many places; here it is possible only to emphasize some of the key points.

Unusually for his time, Arensberg emphasized the study of communal customs and behaviours rather than archaeological remains. The integration of the individual into the community and the maintenance of relations within the group took centre stage in his approach. The functional, systematic aspect of group life became Arensberg's focus as he charted the work done by a family to maintain a small farm. Human beings are shown always to be acting in relation to the built environment and to the animals with which they share their habitat. In this view, the family is an operational unit that thrives on division of labour and predictable allocation of tasks within a tightly organized social and environmental ecology. Skills are not so much taught as learned from parents in the act of performing necessary agricultural tasks; as Arensberg asserts, 'There are no rules to learn that the countryman does not feel within himself or his fellows.'[36] The

Plate 3.   Ray McAnally as the Bull.

particularities of inheriting land, matchmaking, achieving adulthood, delegating familial authority and ownership, thatching or slating the dwelling, co-operating with neighbours, running the household, rearing children, conducting business in shop and pub, and dealing with death all feature in Arensberg's interpretation of the communal dynamism and the nested patterns of local activity that he foregrounds. What Arensberg calls the 'habitual apparatus' of life in a given community is his elusive but compelling object.

No ethnographic description of life in Ireland has ever been uncontroversial. Arensberg's 1930s depiction, although it remains a textual touchstone for those seeking to understand Irish rural experience, is no exception to the rule, and critiques of his claims are many. In fact, although Arensberg's model remains enormously useful for thinking about the Bull's motivations, assumptions and behaviour, *The Field* like many of Keane's plays, may usefully be viewed as a sardonic response to familism.

Historian Joseph Lee views Arensberg's *Irish Countryman* as evidence that hegemonic forces were able to turn what was actually catastrophic rural decline into a depiction of a static, stable society 'at peace with itself'. This was, he claims, a 'highly selective social construction of reality'[37] that held force until the 1950s and 1960s, when the contradiction between the model and lived experience was too great to be accepted even by anthropologists. Donna Birdwell-Pheasant agrees that Arensberg's Ireland 'seems to float in a timeless void, isolated from the perturbations of modern history and disconnected from any meaningful cultural linkage with Ireland's Gaelic and British past'.[38] On the other hand, some researchers have insisted that Arensberg did witness a community that was strong and self-sustaining but that the local economy and social structure were of fairly recent vintage. Far from being an ancient system that had proven itself through an extensive and fraught history, the small family farm as perceived by Arensberg might better be viewed as a rather brief historical interlude within large patterns of cyclic change.

Certainly by the middle of the twentieth century the western counties were in substantial decline as farming centres. In Ireland, as elsewhere in the world, small farmers were being forced out by larger producers and by modernizing processes of consolidation. The de Valera ideal of Irish rural harmony and purity, part and parcel of Irish national identity in the twenties, was eroding significantly by the time that Keane depicts. The contradictions within the system ultimately outstripped its ability to stretch and contain them.

While Arensberg perhaps inevitably misjudged the longitudinal stability of the world he was sketching, he rightly insisted on the fact that the County Clare community was a system. He describes his book as 'an introduction to Irish life and to Irish rural custom and to the interwoven causes and effects explaining the cultural system, the work, the family life, the loyalties, and the values connecting them'.[39] The functionalism that Arensberg espoused finds its contested completion in the works of Keane, who is at pains to probe both the integrity of the social system and the breakdowns attendant on social change.

One important aspect of familism, portrayed by Keane's depiction of how the Bull's extended family assists him, is that the system thrives only as long as alliances are maintained and strengthened over time through marriage. In the view of both Arensberg and Keane, individual identity depends on a communal notion of subjectivity, and social justice is determined within the landscape of extended familial and work-based friendships. Ownership of land is often indistinguishable from community status, which many of Keane's characters view as the ultimate value. Disputes over land ownership resonate in every social interaction.

Keane's work gives force to Arensberg's observation that 'The solidarity of . . . family is strengthened through competition with other socio-economic units. The endless petty disputes of the countryside over rights of way, boundaries, cattle trespasses, drainages, are much more than defences of property. . . . That solidarity is a mountain of strength against the outside world'.[40] The intimidation and murder of William Dee by the Bull and Tadhg, as well as their almost effortless coercion of the local community in hiding their crime, bear witness to the power of familism both historical and imagined.

In his best novel, *The Bodhrán Makers* (1986), Keane shows precisely and unselfconsciously that an entire, intact community with its own sense of tradition (whether recent or ancient) is needed to provide the field of operations in which the act of making and playing a bodhrán has meaning. When the social fabric begins to unravel, when the moral authority vested in the church has been gainsaid, when the local traditions of exchange are eroded, the social structure is ruined and a large portion of the local population spontaneously emigrates to England. However, during the time that Keane portrays in *The Field*, the family still functions as a unit, both in the town of Carraigthomond and in the mountainy lands that host the Bull McCabe's farm. In the play, Leamy's desire to reveal the truth to the authorities and to adhere to a church-sanctioned view of morality marks a moment of instability in this system but does not yet signal its utter breakdown.

2

FIELDWORK: A PRACTICE APPROACH TO FILM

Among other things, ethnomethodology is the study of social practices, and it is useful to compare the work of Pierre Bourdieu with Arensberg's work on Ireland, particularly as we negotiate the move between Keane's play and Sheridan's film based on that drama. Bourdieu wants to work out a sociology of practices. His distinctive turn towards customary behaviours addresses the classic, deep dualisms played out in twentieth-century philosophy and ethnography: subject and object, individual and system. Starting an analysis from attention to practices means seeing both individuality and social structure emerging out of ongoing, shared, routine activity, precisely the sort of background activity that Keane's characters take for granted.

Among the more revealing of Bourdieu's comments on his own anthropological work is a passage in *The Logic of Practice* (1990) in which he describes his efforts to tabulate in one diagram all the variants in the structuring oppositions of traditional life among Algerian peasants. Mapping onto a single chart rites of cooking, planting, the life cycle, the periods of the day, going out and coming in, and other recurrent activities led to 'countless contradictions' that could not be resolved back into fundamental oppositions. His fieldwork, that is, resisted the structuralist management of dichotomies that he had expected to discover in traditional Kabyle life. His synopsis of this cultural evidence showed him the need for a logic of social practices grounded in the notion of what he called a 'generative *habitus*'.

Defining this 'habitus' is tricky, because so much of it operates in the background of a given social field. The habitus is actually a system 'that operates from within agents, though it is neither strictly individual nor in itself fully determinative of conduct'.[41] In a sense, the habitus can be represented by the metaphoric position of a tangler who is caught up in bargains controlled ultimately by the buyer and seller while also exerting pressure on the outcome of the transaction. A given negotiation will always offer challenges to the sense of how things are done. That very know-how cannot always be fully specified but remains partly habitual – embodied by the actor and embedded in the behaviours and systems that make up the society. The habitus, then, offers resistance to outright changes in collective practices; it is essentially conservative. But the routine background activities of any given group are not strong enough to rule out any and all social change or adaptational improvisation as circumstances demand. We might say that the habitus represents a flow of behaviours that interlock to form the character and texture of a culture within a given historical period.

Bourdieu took the term 'habitus' most immediately from Erwin Panofsky's *Gothic Architecture and Scholasticism* (1951).[42] For Panofsky, the concept signifies the ideological categories and assumptions that human beings embody without articulating, possibly without being able to make explicit. This aspect of reality is behavioural rather than intellectual, everyday rather than extraordinary, structural rather than idiosyncratic. As Bourdieuian commentator Richard Jenkins explains:

> the objective world in which groups exist, and the objective environment – other people and things – as experienced from the point of view of individual members of the group, is the product of the past practices of this generation and previous generations . . . Here we have a process of production, a process of adjustment, and a dialectical relationship between collective history inscribed in objective conditions and the habitus inscribed in individuals.[43]

The habitus always stands in dialogue with the often strategic, improvisational, fluid behaviour of individuals who perform tasks not only in space but also over time.[44]

Repeated behaviours, routines learned by children brought up within those activities, habitual and untheorized skills, routine sociation, taken-for-granted structuring mechanisms, uninterrogated kinetic knowledge, post-dualistic human-world interfaces – such terms are used by a wide variety of writers on 'practice' theory, from Anthony Giddens to Andrew Pickering, from Jeff Coulter to Stephen Turner. The effort to account fully for an individual's style, or for a society's symmetries and dissymmetries, leads many of these writers, following Bourdieu, to appreciate the simultaneous overdetermination and underdetermination of social realities and of the fact that 'mastery of this logic is only possible for someone who is completely mastered by it, who possesses it, but so much so that he is totally possessed by it'.[45]

The Bull's obsession with the field and all of the agricultural routines associated with it exemplifies this kind of ingrained behaviour. When we compare Keane's play to Sheridan's film, the first thing we notice is that Sheridan systematically insinuates the Bull into the locale through all kinds of routine activity (praying at the holy well, fertilizing the land, grazing his livestock, tending, renting, making hay). In contrast, Keane obliquely suggests this network of behaviours when he sets up the relations between the Bull and the Bird, the inside and the outside, men's worlds and women's worlds. At the same time, the film of *The Field*, again in contrast to the play, shows us the Bull's coming to consciousness of his habitus – all that he has taken for granted and left relatively unanalyzed. Nigel Floyd points to the 'moment of startling clarity' when the Bull shouts, 'Curse my mother and my father for tying me to the famine field.'[46] Sheridan ups the ante by exaggerating, extravagantly, the practices as well as the resistances bruited within Keane's relatively understated play.

A practice approach offers a sophisticated logic for integrating cultural studies materials into cinema studies. From its inception, cinema has been fascinated by the projection of culturally constitutive activities – for their own sake – on the screen. Our delight in our customary processes of doing and our pleasure in seeing others' habitual doings, especially in close-up, exceeds an atomistic attention to props, people, lights and the paraphernalia of filmmaking. And it is this simple energy – an aspect of film that is rarely discussed – that powers much of Sheridan's film work. He has always emphasized the everyday practices of a given setting. Certainly, the close-up possibilities of film transcend the representational possibilities of stage drama for investigating improvisational practice and diurnal behaviour. In *The Field*, Sheridan and his cinematographer, Jack Conroy, revel in the fact that film depicts everyday practices in gratifying ways.

Before we turn to the film itself, it is useful to comment further on the presentation of practices in Sheridan's unpublished screenplay (September 1989). For instance, Sheridan describes in some detail the gathering of seaweed for fertilizing the field:

> *From a bird's eye perspective we see the two men working. They are collecting seaweed left by the tide. They work quickly, sorting the good from the bad and arranging it into two large piles. The younger man digs his pitchfork into the smaller pile and the older man helps him to hump it onto his back. It is a huge effort.*[47]

Here we get a sense of the men's embodied and ritualized relations to their environment.

Later, Sheridan lingers over the Bull's morning devotions and Tadhg's response to them:

> *Small stone built church. In its protection, the father praying. Deep intense prayer. We can hear the son approach, but the father does not flinch. The son comes running out of the clouds and rushes to the shade of the church. He leans with his back against it and looks down at his father praying. He is out of breath. Slowly, he slips down along the church wall until he sits beside his father. His father makes the sign of the cross and moves on with his pile. Before he turns the corner, he looks back at his son. When his father is gone, the son takes a tiny fag-end from his top pocket and lights*

it. He leaves the small stone church. Hold for a moment.
(Screenplay, p. 3)

We have the feeling that this sequence of events has happened before, and happened often. Each man knows what the other will do. In both of these instances, Sheridan requires the camera to record the ease or difficulty with which these people fit into their world. A feeling of daily routine grows from these descriptions and of varying degrees of acquiescence and resistance to normative activity.

Similarly, we are given a 'close on' view of Mrs McCabe serving dinner:

> THE BULL's *wife taking potatoes off the fire. She brings them to the table. They are boiling hot and the water almost spills as she makes her way to the table. Neither of the men move to help.* THE BULL *stares straight ahead [while]* TADHG *seems concerned but unable to help. She sets the potatoes out on each plate. She gives* THE BULL *three potatoes, he nods for more, four, he nods again, five. He cuts his hand across the food to indicate enough. Throughout the dinner not one word is spoken* [Plate 4]. *It is like a silent movie.* THE BULL *looks at* TADHG *and points to the salt.* TADHG *nods to his mother who picks it up and hands it to his father.* THE BULL *takes a pinch while* TADHG *holds it.*
> (Screenplay, p. 6)

It is not just the miracle of film nor merely the conventions of the cinema that lead Sheridan into such detail in his script. Rather, the writer takes pains to visualize the routine behaviours that would have developed out of the prolonged silence between the Bull and his wife – an unusual deviation from the domestic norm but one in the midst of which they have improvised a transactional ritual. Underlying the director's creative challenge is the fact that Sheridan often films people eating and drinking, whether in prison, as in *In the Name of the Father* (1993), or at the local pub, as in *My Left Foot* (1989), or in

Plate 4.   Dining in silence.

more talkative familial circumstances as in *The Boxer* (1997). In each case the style of eating suits the setting and displays the embodied aspects of the habitus conveyed in dining behaviours. From such minutiae of the everyday Sheridan builds the life-world of each filmed narrative.

When he reimagined Keane's play, Sheridan moved much of the action out of the pub into the townland; at the same time, he created a finely grained and closely choreographed narrative in which each figure has a place and each gesture a practical consequence. Sheridan seems to want to indicate the vanishing point where 'acting' and 'behaviour' converge. While Sheridan's version of the Bull has not pleased all viewers, there can be no doubt that the cinematic Bull has a definite air of practical mastery in relation to family, home, land, cattle and business transactions. His everyday rituals are not choices for him, and he is a tragic figure only insofar as he shows himself unable to make strategic accommodations to an emergent cultural paradigm.

SHERIDAN AND *THE FIELD*

Jim Sheridan in Context

Jim Sheridan (Plate 5) was born in 1949 and grew up in northside Dublin. His family life during the 1960s is impressionistically rendered in his brother Peter Sheridan's memoir *44: Dublin Made Me* (1999). Jim Sheridan attended University College, Dublin, where he read English literature, philosophy and history. Sheridan was eighteen years old when the Project Arts Centre was launched 'as a radical response to limited and traditional values and outlets' such as the revered Abbey Theatre. In 1977 the Sheridan brothers founded the Project Theatre Company, which included Liam Neeson and Gabriel Byrne, and took 'Irish theatre by storm'.[48] Only

Plate 5. Jim Sheridan.

four years later, Jim Sheridan and his family emigrated to New York City so that he could assume the post of artistic director for the Irish Arts Centre under the direction of Nye Heron.

One of Sheridan's hallmarks as a director has been a less-than-reverent treatment of Irish classics in a style that critiqued the Abbey Theatre and its stylized folk realism. Like the Druid Theatre, Sheridan insisted that romantic Ireland be abandoned, or at least firmly bracketed by other views. Gabriel Byrne recalls that, during the seventies, Sheridan 'create[d] a rumpus at the Edinburgh International Festival by starting Yeats's *Purgatory* in the middle. The actors finished the play and then went back to the beginning. "He was saying, that was the point of purgatory, that there's no beginning and end to it."'[49] One suspects that Sheridan was also eager to extricate Irish theatre from the prolonged purgatory of restaging the classics instead of reimagining them.

That noted, in several interviews Sheridan has indicated that the move to New York forced him to question his urge to deconstruct the theatrical mythos. Irish-American audiences preferred their Irish theatre straight. This experience of retooling and recasting has strongly affected Sheridan's filmmaking, which constantly thematizes the relations of theatre and film, of romanticism and realism, of celebration and send-up.

Certainly, the experience of producing plays in New York prepared Sheridan to address the crucial American movie market. Sheridan has noted, 'How we think is conditioned by Hollywood film,'[50] and it would seem that the Hollywood influence furthered Sheridan's theatrical and cinematic remaking of Keane's day and play. In any event, it was the theatre impresario Noel Pearson who invited Sheridan back to Dublin to work on the movie of Christy Brown's autobiographical *My Left Foot*. With only a brief film production course at New York University under his belt, Sheridan co-wrote the script with Shane Connaughton and then directed the film, which garnered Oscars for Daniel Day Lewis (Best Actor) and Brenda

Fricker (Best Actress). Following the triumphs of 1989, Sheridan returned to work, adapting Keane's *The Field* to the screen.

It is quite a leap from the published text of the play to the lush cinematography and settings of Jim Sheridan's film, which follows a script so different as to seem at first glance another work entirely. Nevertheless, the Mercier text of Barnes's edition of Keane was published as a paperback graced with the figure of Richard Harris as Bull McCabe on the front. On the back is a reduced-size poster from the Granada film:

From the Award Winning Team of
'MY LEFT FOOT'
Richard Harris in His Finest Screen Performance
THE FIELD
It owns him. It possesses him.
It could even destroy him.

It was good marketing all round for Granada to allow the use of the promotional materials for the film in marketing Keane's text, but the fact remains that the relation between what Keane wrote (and Barnes edited) and what Sheridan's actors perform is, at best, oblique. Sheridan's unpublished screenplay states clearly that it is 'based upon the play', not congruent with the play.

The mythology surrounding the film has it that when Ray McAnally approached Noel Pearson about producing the play in which he had so famously starred during the 1960s, McAnally was in possession of a filmscript for that purpose. Pearson reports that they were dissatisfied with this version, and so a further version was prepared by Sheridan. Even this screenplay is not precisely what was filmed. Paddy Woodworth has claimed that Sheridan 'used to rewrite his plays hours before they opened at the Project Arts Centre'.[51] Writing about the shooting of *In the Name of the Father*, Michael Dwyer emphasizes Sheridan's predilection for filming scenes in sequence; he quotes Arthur Lappin, who says that Sheridan 'tends to be using the script more as a skeleton . . . and there has been a huge amount of enhancement of the script on the actual day of filming'.[52] It is likely that a certain amount of seat-of-the-pants improvisation took place among Sheridan, his actors and the cinematographer during the filming in Leenane, County Mayo, and during the editing process for *The Field*.

This complicated textual history mandates that we be quite specific about the structure of the film and its considerable deviations from the Keane text in tone, character, setting and action. Whereas Keane's play adheres to the conventions of Irish drama in placing most of the action indoors, Sheridan insists on opening the story to its roots in the countryside. We see the Bull (Richard Harris) and his son Tadhg (Sean Bean) working the land and tending to their home, at the outdoor auction and at chapel. Sheridan introduces a scene in which the Bull is replacing the thatched roof with slate, a traditional way of making the parental home look more affluent as the desired matchmaking for Tadhg draws near. We are also given glimpses of life within the Bull's family. Rather than merely being told that McCabe and his wife (Brenda Fricker) have not spoken for many years, we witness the silent mealtimes and stultifying demeanour of this family at odds with itself. Echoing that adversarial tone, Sheridan transforms the Bull's relationship with the Widow (Frances Tomelty). In place of the cheerful Maggie, we have the stiff, formal female who, unknown to the Bull, has suffered years of harassment from Tadhg and the Bird (John Hurt).

The tensions between the Bull and these women suffuse his emotional life with incomprehension and fuel his desire to find Tadhg a good wife. Extending that theme, Sheridan introduces scenes in which the Bull consults the local matchmaker, Dan Paddy Andy, played by the playwright's brother, Eamon Keane. The matchmaker is a recurrent figure in Keane's world, and within the world of the film the practice of arranging matches dovetails with the Bird's activities, which in Sheridan's film hover somewhere between those of a tangler and those of a foolhardy meddler, as well as with those of the local travelling people.

The familist activity of matchmaking informs a striking, disturbing scene that is not suggested by the play. Where Keane posits Tadhg's independent scouting of a local woman to marry, Sheridan has the Bull notice that Tadhg is attracted to a travelling woman and contact Andy, who encourages the Bull to come with Tadhg to 'a Wake celebration for the young men and women who are going to America and England' (Screenplay, p. 32). When a local laments the loss of the young people, Andy replies, 'The land can only support so many, that's the lesson of the famine' (Screenplay, p. 32). Beyond this clear and guiding principle, the scene is laden with entanglements of all kinds.

For instance, as the American who has come to buy the field, Peter (Tom Berenger), enters the dancehall, both the Bull and Tadhg track him with their gaze. Meanwhile, a travelling woman 'steals the Bird's drink. Peter becomes aware of Tadhg's eyes on him. He smiles at Tadhg. No response. The Bull and the Bird watch the interplay between Tadhg and the American' (Screenplay, p. 32). At this point the Bull asks Andy to point out the woman that he has in mind for Tadhg, and the traveller, known in the screenplay as the Red Head (Jenny Conroy), walks onto the dance-floor by herself. A boy asks Tadhg to join them and 'come to Philadelphia' the following morning. Tempted, Tadhg is taunted by the boy, who says, 'You'll end up like the Bird, Tadhg' (Screenplay, p. 33). The Red Head challenges the men to dance with her, and says, 'Are you all afraid of me? The tinker's daughter. You're all afraid that if you touch me you'll lose the soil under your feet and end up sleeping under the stars.' Trying to draw out 'the biggest man among you' (Screenplay, p. 34), she captures Tadhg's attention until the Bull, sensing his son's desire, grabs her hand. Meanwhile, the Yank is about to dance with the McRoarty girl (Sara Jane Scaife), who is intended to be Tadhg's match, until the Bull weaves together the Yank and the traveller, placing Miss McRoarty in Tadhg's hands. It transpires that the Yank

Plate 6. Tadhg and the Yank face off.

has 'Irish blood in him all right' (Screenplay, p. 35), at least judging by his ability to dance in the local fashion. As complicated as sorting out dance partners has been, the dancing is even more engrossing and entangling.

As the music speeds up, Tadhg and the American compete, and the crowd shouts for more (Plate 6). Sheridan writes:

> *We are in the middle of some primal wild exorcism. The atmosphere changes from abandon to something more serious. . . . The music is furious.* THE BIRD *demented, like a mad figure from Bosch, he spins, pouring drink on his head.* THE BULL *calls for the dance to go faster . . .* THE RED HEAD *is obviously enjoying herself, wanting to push the madness further.* (Screenplay, p. 36)

She becomes 'abandoned' and 'witch like'. In the screenplay, the Yank becomes as 'demented' and 'animal'-like as the Bird and Tadhg; in the film, however, it is the Bull who calls things to a halt when he sees that the McRoarty girl cannot stand the pressure of Tadhg's spinning. In both script and film, Sheridan has lavished attention on this scene. The screenplay describes minutely the frantic spinning of the dancers:

> *From* TADHG's *P.O.V. we see* PETER's *face spinning through the frame, every second or so.* PETER *seems to be going faster.* TADHG *digs his heels in, trying to keep control and to go faster. We see in close up, a huge gargantuan effort from* TADHG. *He stares at* PETER. PETER's *face spins so fast now that it seems set in place, a memory from a nightmare fixed terrifyingly there, just beyond our reach.* (Screenplay, p. 36)

In this spectacular scene, we find the communal activity of dancing standing in for traditional mores in general, and we see that tradition challenged in several ways. First, most of those who are dancing will be leaving the next day for America or England. Further, as one who has rejected the land, the travelling woman brings a premonitory dread into the proceedings. Finally, Tadhg is not able to keep up with the admired Yank in his apparently flawless execution of his inborn Irishness, and when he tries to do so, he symbolically violates his partner and destroys the rhythm of the dance. Tadhg's running from the hall in shame is part of his general pattern of running away. More importantly, the social confusion that occurs in this scene expresses a gothic primitivism that Sheridan indulges in throughout the screenplay. One reading of this crucial scene is that this rural townland has to work harder and harder to keep its fundamental practices in focus. What may at times appear to be elegant and spontaneous execution of the old ways – whether matchmaking, tangling, dancing or allocating land – is literally spinning out of control and thereby unleashing dark forces previously only barely reined in by traditional behaviours and familist social organization.

To get to this point of breakdown, Sheridan significantly complicates the depiction of Tadhg. In productions of the play, Tadhg has been imagined at various points along a spectrum from enthusiastic clone of his father to somewhat resistant but cowed servant of the land. In the film, Tadhg is sullen and stubbornly dim. He resists his father's efforts to find him a wife; instead, he is helplessly drawn to the Red Head, whom the film calls the 'tinker's daughter'. She chides, teases and lures Tadhg; he watches her and follows her lead. After the death of the outsider, Tadhg goes to the woman's bed, and the young couple decide to leave Carraigthomond. From that split between the Bull and his son comes the startling conclusion to Sheridan's story. The Bull descends into madness; the Bird calls Tadhg back from his journey to stop the Bull driving their livestock into the sea; Tadhg is swept over the cliff with the livestock (Plate 7); and his father expands into a mixture of Cuchulainn and Canute – semi-mythic figures from the mists of Anglo-Irish history. The Bull ineffectually fights to keep the waves away from the body of his son.

Not content with this significant complication and melo-dramatization of the play, Sheridan also introduced the shadow of Séimí, Tadhg's older brother, who had killed himself many years earlier. The parental alienation in the film has resulted not, as in Keane's play, from Mrs McCabe's allowing a tinker's pony to graze on their land but rather from the Bull's refusal, now eighteen years on, to allow Séimí's name to be mentioned in the home. In addition, Sheridan replaced the anglified William Dee with the stereotypical figure of the Returned Yank, thereby moving the conflict from the colonial matrix to that of American commercial imperialism.

A further, crucial change from the play to the film involves the depiction of women. The women we see in Keane's play are complex and also fairly sympathetic figures. Keane's widow auctions off her four-acre field to supplement her pension; although she asserts her right to sell to the highest bidder, she need not be played as the harassed, angry and vindictive figure of the film. Keane's publican has a feisty but long-suffering wife, Maimie, who chafes at the town's 'squinting windows' habits and sadly registers the impact on her son

Plate 7. Familism in ruins.

Leamy of the duplicities he witnesses in the pub. Keane gives us a glimpse of a McCabe woman married to the Bull's cousin Dandy; the Bull requires them to vouch for him on the night of the murder, but Dandy's wife enacts an entirely comic role.

These standard theatrical types, all more or less comfortable in the play's pub setting, shapeshift into Sheridan's terrorized and embittered widow, the silently brooding wife and the glamorous, provocative travelling woman of the film. While the play maintains a traditional patriarchal social order and brackets female agency, the film both opens up and complicates the social roles available to women. The mixed piety, strength and endurance possessed by the Bull's wife coexist with the widow's severe presence and the freedom from historical obsessions signalled by the tinker's daughter.

Plate 8. The Bird.

Note the scene in which the widow (Plate 9) comes to the pub to register her land with the publican-auctioneer. (This transcription of the dialogue from the film is my own. In square brackets, I have included passages from the screenplay to indicate the effects that Sheridan's written stage directions produce.)

Laughter in pub. Silence as [THE WIDOW] *enters.* '[*The* WIDOW] *comes through the door. It is like a visit of an alien*' (Screenplay, p. 9).]

> PUBKEEPER: Can't serve you at this hour, ma'am.
>
> WIDOW: I don't want a drink. I want to sell the field.

['*All the men watch the* WIDOW. *On the mention of the word "Field" it is as if she wanted to sell her virginity. The shop has become tense*' (Screenplay, p. 10).]

> PUBKEEPER: The field?
>
> WIDOW: Aye, the field. I need the best price I can get.

Plate 9. The Widow.

BIRD: Bull McCabe's field?

WIDOW: He rents it.

MAN AT BAR: 'Twas bare rock when he got it, ma'am.

SECOND MAN: *Ominously.* Barren.

THIRD MAN (pubkeeper?): He broke it into a lovely field.

WIDOW: 'Twill go to the highest bidder.

General silence.

BIRD: Bidder?

WIDOW: 'Twill be sold by public auction.

['*The* WIDOW *has touched a nerve here. Most of the farmers watch in stunned, stone cold silence, as if touched by memory of a loss too deep for words. The land is in these people's souls. The tinkers snigger to themselves*' (Screenplay, p. 11).]

MAN: You've no right to sell the field.

WIDOW: It's my land. I'll take my chances. 'Twill be sold by public auction on October the first. Whoever pays the most gets the field.

['The men look at her as if she were offering sexual favours, with a mixture of excitement and disgust. The tinkers happy at the misfortune of the settled people' (Screenplay, p. 11).]

WIDOW: I'm washing my hands of that field.

She leaves the pub.

Although the Bull insists that the crowd treat the Widow with respect, it is his own son who acts out the mixed emotions of patriarchy towards women. As well as falling in love with an unsuitable girl, Tadhg has joined with the Bird in antagonizing the Widow for the decade after her husband's death. The Bird and Tadhg treat the Widow as secret societies did landlords. Their 'Captain Moonlight' activities echo the 'outrages' that accompanied land war and legislative battles – burning out landlords, destroying crops, boy-cotting. The programme of intimidation to which Tadhg and the Bird subject the Widow differs little from that to which the Bull subjects the Yank.

What makes these actions so troubling is that they rest on the local, counter-institutional ethics that the Bird practises and enables for the community in his role as tangler. As John Hurt campily performs the Bird, his abject state signifies this double-mindedness (Plate 8). At the same time, the Bird is intimately a part of the familial body: he tells Tadhg that the infant Séimí was like a lump on his back. Thus, the Bird represents the weaknesses inherent in familism. And he persists in all manner of entangling activity. At one point, he rashly intimates to the tinkers that the Bull and Tadhg disposed of their donkey. Later, in his constant effort to gather information that he may be able to trade, the Bird spies on the Bull as he kills the Yank. Later still, when the Bird tells the Bull that Tadhg is with the tinker's daughter and announces to Tadhg that his father is driving the cattle to the cliffs, the Bird's meddling produces disastrous consequences. This feature of the Bird is an extrapolation on Sheridan's part from the more restrained and delimited trading practices that Keane's character embodies. In

Sheridan's hands, the Bird was dangerous from the outset. The screenplay presents him spying on the Bull and Tadhg as they dump the donkey into the lake; he steals potatoes and a chicken that Tadhg leaves for the tinker's daughter; he eavesdrops on a conversation between Tadhg and the travelling woman while the Bull sells some milch cows. The Bird becomes a metonym for the social disruptions and surveillance culture that characterized Ireland in the eighties.

Partly because of the extensive changes to the play, reviewers of the film were divided. In the *Irish Times*, Michael Dwyer asserts that Sheridan 'lives up to the great promise' of *My Left Foot*. Dwyer praises the director for 'a firm narrative assurance' and the extension of his 'considerable cinematic skills'. He detects only one 'false note' in the film, the scene in which the Bird is chased down the road to the sound of a traditional jig.[53] A contrasting view was presented by Johnny Gogan in Ireland's *Film Base News*. Gogan states that 'the film fails to realise its own epic claims'. He finds Tadhg 'poorly realised' and confusingly played to emphasize the son's apparent 'idiocy'. Similarly, Brenda Fricker fails to negotiate the move from the wife's long silence to her communicating with the Bull. On the other hand, he applauds John Hurt's full portrayal of the Bird and Tom Berenger's 'stylized' Yank. The 'central disappointment', Gogan finds, is that 'many powerful and evocative things are said – mostly by The Bull – but they are rarely seen and less felt'. Ultimately, Gogan finds the film derivative and 'rootless'.[54] Many Irish reviewers registered positive readings, although they had reservations regarding characterization, stereotyping, allegorization, derivativeness and generalized Oirishry.

In Britain, the *Guardian* reviewer Derek Malcolm found the film strong on 'conviction' and acting but compromised by 'clichés'; he comments, 'When the Irish put something on the screen, it seems almost to stay there intact and defy gravity.'[55] He notes, too, the problem of scale in the film; Harris being conceived as larger than life while the other characters occupy lesser stations. By the same token, Christopher Tookey observes in the *Sunday Telegraph*, 'The real problem is a script which can't sustain a performance of this size'. Aiming for mythic resonance, Harris sometimes gets 'bogged down in Great Acting'.[56] Similarly, the reviewer for *The Times*, noting that John B. Keane is 'a man much garlanded on his home turf', objects to the 'stage machinery' visible in the film. 'At peak moments', he states, 'the dialogue collapses into declamatory clumps', and the characters 'obstinately remain actors acting'.[57] In contrast, Nigel Floyd argues in the *Monthly Film Bulletin* that Sheridan avoids the pitfalls of symbolism and 'tragic gestures in favour of a more intimate concern with the fabric of Irish rural life'.[58]

On the American front, Roger Ebert also objects to the staginess of the performances. 'This was not', he says, 'a work that called out to be filmed. Once filmed, it calls out to be forgotten'.[59] Writing for the *Washington Post*, Rita Kempley asserts that, in contrast to *My Left Foot*, Sheridan 'seems out in left field here, undone by the sheer hokum of the material'.[60] And *Rolling Stone* says, 'Audiences are less likely to choose sides than flee from the overacting of Harris and John Hurt as his dimwitted crony. Sometimes gorgeous scenery is just not enough'.[61]

Although some reviewers clearly had not read Keane's play or had forgotten how different it is from the film version, others pointedly objected to the accretions around the playscript. In discussing the transition from Keane's play to Sheridan's film, Irish film historian Kevin Rockett asserts that only two of the changes to the play were 'crucial' – the shift from William Dee to the Yank and the change in time from the 1960s to the 1930s. Rockett sees these changes as watering down 'the impact of the film', changes 'made for quite particular reasons' that 'were effectively forced on the production by the film's backers'.[62] It is Rockett's suspicion that these backers wanted to emphasize the pre-modernity of Irish rural life, skirting the heady transitional sixties in doing so, and including an American actor to heighten the appeal of the film for US and British audiences. At the same time, Rockett acknowledges that in 1990 the film 'became the first Irish-produced film, for which evidence exists, to top the box-office ratings' in Ireland itself.[63] At a cost of only IR£4.5 million (€ 5.7 million) and 'exclusively funded by British television',[64] *The Field* was nevertheless partially tailored to meet external requirements for getting the film made.

In what appears to be a riposte to Rockett's suggestion that the film was overly influenced by foreign parties, producer Noel Pearson has emphasized that Granada alone funded the film – the suggestion being that Granada was not beholden to American interests. Pearson goes on to explain changes to the play as simply aspects of the drama's adaptation for the movies.[65] While some degree of spin is to be expected in such retrospective views, Pearson's larger aim is to defend the artistic integrity of the film, including its turn from an English interloper to an American bidder for the field and the film's chronological resetting. Certainly the provisional acceptance of this defence brings some interesting elements of the film and its genesis into view.

Bracketing the issue of historical period, one can observe that, within Sheridan's film-driven and often ironic imagination, the portrayal of an American outsider enabled overt references to movies like *The Quiet Man* (dir. John Ford, 1952) or even the earlier *The Luck of the Irish* (dir. Henry Koster, 1948). Tom Berenger's characterization has much of the laconic stoicism and lumpen bemusement of John Wayne's famous role in the John Ford film. By the same token, the arrival in Carraigthomond of Sheridan's Yank in a speeding motorcar and the subsequent immobilization of that vehicle by a flat tyre evokes *The Luck of the Irish*, in which the similarly trench-coated American finds his car sinking in a river.

What Berenger brought to the role of the American, besides a generic Stateside aura, was his own analysis of the Yank's motivation. Interviewed during filming, Tom Berenger said, 'I had a little bit of a problem with the character at first. There should be a sense of mystery about him, but I went to Jim and said, "I just need a couple more specifics on the guy.'" The interviewer adds, 'Later, the historically inclined Berenger provided the character with a past of his own invention. "I figure he's got an office in Dublin and one in Boston. It's 1939, and they're using a lot of concrete for highways and for the lend-lease ships. He says he wants to build a factory, but he's also here because his family is from the area. But he doesn't really *need* the field – that's his problem."'[66] The method-inspired Berenger saw his character as flawed and perhaps, therefore, as doomed.

Several reviewers found Berenger's portrayal wooden, but another reading is that the American actor meant to project the Yank's more profound inability to grasp the nature of the Bull's involvement with the land. The Yank is constructed in such a way that he can be viewed entirely as a representative of capitalism's evil empire. His presence signals the cumulative impact of economic change on Irish life in the second half of the twentieth century. From the time of the seventies' international oil crisis onwards, the changes in Irish culture were dramatic, and intellectual debate over the displacement of tradition by modernity – for good or ill – became a salient feature of this persistent and escalating social change. One argument of this essay is that the film of *The Field* is most interesting as a document of life in eighties Ireland; its layered and disjunctive form speaks most eloquently not about Keane's area of concern – the mid century in which he lived and whose mores he depicted – but rather about the pace and nature of change in social practices during the eighties. Characteristically, Sheridan intensifies his source material and the contrast with his own era by relocating the action to 1939, a time whose *Quiet Man* traditionalism sets up an optimal contrast with the conditions of Irish life that Sheridan was experiencing in the 1980s.

Sheridan's writing strategy seems to have involved persistently asking 'what if?' What if we take the Keane story, hold onto its proto-cinematic attention to practices and magnify its disruptions on the basis of attitudes shared by the youth of late-twentieth-century rural and urban Ireland? What if, at an aesthetic level, we retain and embellish the romanticized views of the landscape so often critiqued by Irish intellectuals, while dramatizing the painful instabilities of tending the land? One result is that, whereas Keane adds the reflections of life in the late fifties and early sixties to a sort of Arensberg-based pastiche of the thirties, Sheridan updates this outlook to include the cultural debates of the eighties.

To return to the moment when Ray McAnally handed a script to Noel Pearson is precisely to locate oneself in the mid to late 1980s. Irish society at this time has deeply conflicting views of the Northern Irish crisis, the political future of the island, the prospects for social justice and the government's assiduous courting of multinational investment. Unemployment is reaching an all-time high, and a concentrated cultural despair is in the air. Soon-to-be-Minister of Arts, Culture and the Gaeltacht Michael D. Higgins writes of his generation's sense of 'sharply frustrating limitations on their powers to live fully'.[67] Ireland was confronting not only economic turmoil and the onslaught of modernization but also widespread civil rights agitation, paramilitary violence, the oil crisis, increasing unemployment, feminist activism and a growing understanding of postcolonial trauma. As Sheridan imagines it, Tadhg's desire to leave the land, his inability to 'understand about the land', was shared by thousands of Sheridan's peers.

In response to these cataclysmic changes, Irish intellectuals engaged in extensive cultural debate about evolving aspects of Irishness. Bringing economic, political, sexual and social crises into discourse was the distinctive contribution of *The Crane Bag* (1977–85), a periodical devoted to exploring Irishness in all of its dimensions during this time of extravagant transition. Editors Mark Hederman and Richard Kearney solicited statements from Irish writers and painters, pop musicians and filmmakers, historians and sociologists, philosophers and paramilitaries, feminists and psychologists, to debate the pressing issues of the day, while mapping the terms by which Ireland could move into the twenty-first century. These commentators explored the place of politics and the politics of place, the Irish literary tradition and the multiculturalism of the island, images of women and sectarian stereotypes, travelling people and settled people, discrimination and privilege, the Irish language and English cultural domination, educational initiatives and Irish connections to Eastern Europe, advertising and art, sexualities and changing familial structures. *The Crane Bag* was not the only instrument of concerted social discussion during the late twentieth century in Ireland, but it exemplifies this strand of cultural commentary, not the least in its recurrent flirtation with a psychosocial reading of history.

Certainly, *The Field* as Sheridan rewrote it was profoundly influenced by the psychohistorical reading of Irish cultural traumas – colonization, the Famine, the Troubles – favoured in the era of *The Crane Bag*. Psychohistorical hypotheses surfaced as part of the musings on cultural identity of writers as different as Estyn Evans, Joseph Lee, Vincent Kenny, Fintan O'Toole and Richard Kearney. According to this allegorical reading, during the 1980s the Irish suffered traumas from historical disfranchisements: the loss of land, the loss of language, the disruptions of the Famine and of subsequent migrations. Out of this experience of cultural loss emerged a distinctive collective emotional style, what psychotherapist Vincent Kenny, writing in 1985, memorably called 'the postcolonial personality',[68] a type characterized by distinctively neurotic responses to the environment. Kenny posits a generalized arrested development in Ireland deriving from colonial domination. Sheridan's depiction of Tadhg as strangely conflicted and emotionally stunted fleshes out this conception of developmental stalemate. Another symptom was the development of a complex inner life at the expense of accomplishments in the larger world of international commerce and art. Going underground emotionally included a profound sense of shame at being Irish. According to Kenny, such symptoms could be readily observed in Irish daily life, and it must be acknowledged that his view finds support in Frantz

Fanon's study of colonial wretchedness and its psychic toll.[69] In this postcolonial sociopolitical climate, Irish film tended to be read and received allegorically: the serious debates over cinematic form were less about economic viability in the world marketplace than about the adequacy of movie representations to the changing experience of Irishness in the late twentieth century.

Although the period's approach to national character rapidly reached a dead end, Sheridan's cinematic response to this sometimes inflated debate was both witty and penetrating. At every level of Keane's play, Sheridan enhanced the cinematic nature of the narrative, allowing the lean dramatic outline to open towards multiple sub-plots and side-themes. The psychological stakes are significantly raised in this redaction of the story, and the land moves from being mostly offstage to being lavishly portrayed in classic *Bord Fáilte* (tourist board) fashion. All of these embellishments serve Sheridan's purpose of thematizing the relations between Irish theatre and a once-again emergent Irish cinema. Further, by building on both the practice-oriented dimension of the work and the psychological underpinnings, Sheridan creates a homology between that theatre-to-film development and his characteristic theme of father–son relations. In a very real sense, Irish drama fathers the experiential zone occupied by its cinematic offspring. The director seems to have found much of the Anglo-Irish literary tradition asking to be drawn into the cinematic *mise-en-scène*. This relationship is not without its uneasy and even apocalyptic moments, and the denouement that Sheridan fashions from Keane's quieter drama takes its cues from this enlarged and sometimes overreaching interpretative context.

Father, Son and the Law of the Land

The play's opening scene, with its emphasis on the Bird and Leamy, on Maggie's putting the field up for auction and on the Bull's manipulations to conduct the auction quietly, is entirely different from the film's overture, and yet the emphasis on rural practices, on the texture of familist life, receives even more emphasis from Sheridan. Against a rising sun, two figures and a cart stand silhouetted. At the top of a hill, they toss their bundle into the sea – a dead donkey, whose face we see in close-up as it descends through the water. Underwater, the beast is pale. Much later, the donkey is joined by the dead Yank, whose grey visage is rinsed of all affect as he floats in the lake. But it is the faces of the Bull and Tadhg that hold our attention as they watch the waters swallow the animal. The younger man looks at once thuggish and gratified, while the older man, resplendently patriarchal with his white beard and intelligent attentiveness, appears unsettled and anxious. From the first moment that we see him, the Bull is in denial, trying to hide what he cannot mend.

A cut to the coastline shows the men gathering seaweed. No words have been exchanged yet, the focus remaining on the work in progress. The Bull shows a Bourdieuian fluidity, a true mastery in each of his actions: left to his own devices, he can carry out any of the fundamental practices of his way of life with ease. However, from the outset the son struggles (Plate 10). He seems not to fit into his skin very well, and his discomfort extends to every detail of the opening strophe. While the Bull walks effortlessly uphill, Tadhg stumbles on the rough stones. While the Bull prays at a local shrine, Tadhg sits aside, bored and restless. As they approach the field to deposit their load of seaweed-fertilizer, Tadhg runs recklessly, letting gravity take over, while the Bull strides purposefully towards the treasured piece of land. After this patient cinematic depiction of the methodical father still somewhat amused by his slow-learning but beloved son, the two sit together. They look down on their field and smile. And the Bull states catechistically, 'God made the world. And seaweed made that field, boy.' As the morning unfolds, the Bull pays the Widow her rent, remembering that the anniversary of her husband's death is approaching. He tells her of his desire to see Tadhg settled in marriage. As a sequence, this somewhat ponderous slice of

Plate 10. Tadhg following the Bull.

life conveys the many ways in which the Bull instructs his son in the care of the land.

As Joe Dowling has commented, Sheridan's Bull is like Moses or Job. His Old Testament stoicism is rivalled only by his righteousness. The Bull tells Tadhg, 'Our father's father's father's father dug that soil with their [*sic*] bare hands, made those walls. Our souls is buried down there. And your son's son's son's sons will take care of it, boy. Do you get my meaning?'[70] In the fractured ideologies of eighties Ireland, the meaning tended to be elusive, just as the Bull's statements tend to be comically over-emphatic. An obvious problem with the script when viewed from even a semi-realist point of view is the contradiction between this evocation of a long line of McCabes at work in the field and the clear statement during the scene in which the Widow announces the sale of the field, that this land was 'bare rock' before the Bull reclaimed it with sweat and fertilizer. To give the scriptwriter his due, however, it is clear that, for the Bull, embedded as he is in the ways of the land, tradition is so profound and his relation to the field so all-encompassing as to be almost impossible to historicize. He cannot find the words or the mien sufficient to convey the fundamental necessity of owning property to a son unnaturally ready to abandon the land for a tinker's daughter. From the perspective of a northside-Dublin-born film director in the 1980s, there is something terribly right about the Bull's almost inchoate view of the land.

What makes this film so unsettling is the suggestion that, as far back as 1939, all of the social forces that would make the eighties a time of crisis in Ireland were already detectable in an extreme rural outpost. Despite some ominous psychic notes in the visual orchestration of the opening scenes, everything about the Bull's demeanour and expert execution of local folkways suggests that the seamless reproduction of the familist system will continue unobstructed in the hills around Carraigthomond. Throughout the film, the Bull's purpose remains the same – to improvise a way to bring the everyday back into line with itself. But the experience of the late twentieth century modifies this belief in a traditional status quo.

Sheridan alludes to *Man of Aran* (dir. Robert Flaherty, 1934), a film actually produced in the decade that he is putatively depicting in *The Field*. Despite the fact that the mechanics of lifestyle presented in *Man of Aran* were historically incorrect at the time of filming,[71] Robert Flaherty does convey a powerful habitus, and *The Field* signals from the outset its purchase on a similar terrain. It is evident that the Bull assumes the monumentality of Flaherty's protagonist to emphasize the practical basis of his relation to the land. While the Bull becomes a mythic figure striding purposefully through his accustomed world, his son is just a chancer, locked out of that primal world of pure activity, unable to 'understand about the land'. In fact, we are allowed to see in painful detail that there are not just two laws and two logics, but also two incompatible ways of life – the father's intuitive traditionalism and the son's pre-emptive late-century questioning. The Bull's labour-based purchase on the land makes him part of it and makes the land continuous with his own embodiment, while Tadhg occupies the subject position of the islanders whom Flaherty had to coerce into relearning the old ways for his film.

Like the relation between a stage original and a cinematic rewrite, the terms of the father–son bond are unstable across the course of Irish cinema. Consider that *Man of Aran* opens with a view of a boy catching a shellfish and putting it in his cap. We see how the practices are carried forward, first in the child at play, then in the domestic interior. Everyone is doing, and the doing is relational, intimate, and quite separate from the huge seas that storm into view. The first section of *Man of Aran* addresses the sea, while the second section celebrates farming practices in a landscape stripped of soil. Seaweed-toting, rock-breaking and crevice-searching all contribute to the production of arable land through human agency. Father, son and soil form a single ensemble of production. Practical activity rests on mirroring and cross-generational co-operation.

However, later Irish generations, postwar populations forced to emigrate in search of work, often justifiably felt let down by their parents. Note the passion with which Keane addresses this issue in his autobiography:

> If there is an artist in this country – a real artist who wants to capture the truth for eternity on his canvases – my advice is to go to the North Wall, to Dun Laoghaire, to Rosslare or to Cork. Watch the faces, and, unless you're a heartless inhuman moron, you'll feel something and your conscience will begin to bother you. I have been accused on several occasions of highlighting the problem of emigration and of evading the issue of a solution. The solution is – don't go!

> Stay at home. We are your people and this is your country.
> We – the ones at home – are responsible for you.[72]

Keane wants to convince the older generations that they must assume responsibility for their offspring instead of conditioning their children to emigrate. This outrage at the educated-for-export mentality shapes his masterwork, *The Bodhrán Makers* (1986), which documents the collapse of an entire Irish townland. The waves of emigration during the fifties and sixties inflect Keane's understanding of the Bull's insistence on keeping the land and on maintaining the received practice of sending away all but the first-born son.

The responsibility of one generation for its successors seems to be at the heart of Sheridan's addition of Séimí to the script. We are encouraged to believe that Séimí was so tormented by the fact that his younger brother Tadhg would have to leave the land that many years before the action of the film the older son killed himself. The at first unaddressed question of why Séimí committed suicide is one to which Sheridan compulsively returns. The Bird voices it. Tadhg wonders over it. And the Bull himself keeps struggling internally to figure out what constituted what he sees as the weakness in his first-born. Consider the scene in which Tadhg and the Bull walk down the road to the falls, where they plan to waylay the Yank. The rain has stopped, and in the calm Tadhg broaches the question of why his parents do not converse with each other. Tadhg then asks how old he was when his brother died and adds, 'What age was Séimí?' Badly unsettled by the query, the Bull responds that Séimí was 'thirteen years, six months, and twenty-four days' old at his death.

This heartrending precision, reinforced by the soundtrack's eerie, other-worldly music, signifies the Bull's larger mental instabilities, and occurs just before the Yank's car pulls up at the falls. To the Bull's injunction, 'Be a good Yank. Turn around. Go home', the visitor says that the Bull and Tadhg are breaking the law. Father and son laugh. According to the Bull, his blackthorn stick is 'the law'. Bull first tells

Tadhg to tackle the Yank, but the Yank can box as well as dance, and he easily flattens Tadhg. Bull forces him, insisting that he get up and fight again. His forcing of Tadhg, and his constant registering of the ways in which this son falls short, underscore the reasons for Séimí's withdrawal from life. The Bull experiences shame in his younger son, a shame that echoes in the name of his dead child, taints Tadhg's brief existence and ironically ensures the family's loss of the land and its sustaining folkways.

What is remarkable is how removed from the Bull's practice-centred and familist vision Tadhg is able to be. However often the Bull explains things to him and however fully he has been embedded in these rural practices in a rather isolated everyday, Tadhg's desire has been inscribed elsewhere. For whatever reasons, Tadhg is different from his father, a difference cinematically located in the attractive traveller who wins Tadhg's heart. Both Séimí and Tadhg represent the several Irish generations who discovered that, although they could not be removed from the land without legal machinations, they could remove themselves and seek lives elsewhere. Those generations' pain, shame, guilt, despair, protest and exile echo in the story of the Bull's mysterious offspring.

To produce the atmosphere and storyline of the film, Sheridan combined elements from the stories presented by Keane in his trilogy *Sive*, *The Field* and *Big Maggie*. The familist relations that the Bull's lifestyle promotes, encompassing the running of home and farm, are often depicted by these popular Keane plays as caustic, coercive and abusive. For instance, in Keane's rural Irish homes, there is the constant threat of beating. Big Maggie's domination of her children aims at total control, and her ordering them to cook her meals and meet her needs is entirely in keeping with the Bull's control of Tadhg. Taken as a whole, Keane's trilogy entirely vindicates Lacan's view that the child's desire is the desire of the parents. When the child's desire deviates, there is always hell to pay. In *Big Maggie*, one child is blackmailed into a lucrative marriage, and two of her offspring escape to England. At the same time, Maggie is clear that she has to fend for herself and not allow a daughter-in-law to run her life, as is the case with Mena in *Sive*. Maggie's son Maurice, desperate to marry the woman who is carrying his child, is also distraught at the idea of having to go off with her to England because Maggie won't give them a share of the business: 'You are driving me out of my father's house, out of the home where I was born and reared. I hate going! I hate it! I hate it! I hate it! I'm a grown man and yet I have nothing, no money, no land, no home. Who can I thank for it all? My own mother!'[73]

Keane's children are not equal to their parents' needs. Rather, they are destroyed by the pressures placed on them. Sheridan projects their desperation and entrapment onto the ghostly figure of Séimí, whose name accumulates both predictable and less overt associations in the web of Sheridan's creativity. We have to tease out these associations, beginning with the fact that 'Shea' is the name that Jim Sheridan was called by his birth family.[74] Further, Sheridan's screenplay anglicizes the Irish Séimí as 'Sheamie'. If we view this spelling as a sort of code (Shea equals Me), we discover evidence that the dead son is the locus for Sheridan's own issues as the son of a 'larger-than-life patriarch'.[75]

These issues are illustrated in Sheridan's early play *Mobile Homes*,[76] in which the main character is a newly married young man called Shea. The mobile home that Shea and his wife Ann purchase is trouble from the beginning. It is unhealthy, has hidden fees, lacks electricity, comes with dubious neighbours and is controlled by an oppressive landlord. Shea is handy with socialist rhetoric and has a good sense of how to organize his neighbours to ameliorate these conditions. However, he has problems communicating with his father. When the electricity is turned off in their mobile home, so that Shea and Ann have to move in with Shea's parents, the father relentlessly jeers at Shea for his so-called groucho-marxism. Shea responds by attacking his father's support for Fianna Fáil's policies on unemployment, housing, the North and tax concessions for foreign investment: 'Would you ever look at yourselves in the mirror and see the reflection.'

Immovable, the father objects to the very concept of a mobile home: 'Look, get your feet planted in good soil, otherwise you'll be up to your neck in quicksand.'[77] Portentously, the father tells Shea that he is 'on the precipice now' – a metaphoric version of Tadhg's final encounter with the Bull. As Shea tries to leave, he is told, 'You've got to come face to face with life sometime and it's horrible.' His father strikes him down.[78] Ann tries to quiet the men, but to the father's continued goading Shea responds, 'Look at yourself before you talk about me. Look. *He takes up a mirror.* You're more frightened than me ......Look.' The father's shout, 'no wonder you've nowhere to live', leads to a struggle:

> *Father grabs mirror from him and smashes it off the ground. He then grabs Shea by the neck and holds his face down to one of the fragments.*
>
> FATHER: Look at your image....look....look. That's your generation, shattered in a thousand fucking pieces all over the kip....look. Does it make sense?[79]

In both *Mobile Homes* and *The Field*, masculine generational conflict, domestic disarray and floating shame gather around the image of the mirror and the name of the son.

If Irish writers of Sheridan's generation are to be believed, the father that 1980s emigrants left Ireland to escape was intolerant, atavistic, irascible, at the same time acute and barbarous. Thus, when the father shatters the mirror and forces his son to look at it, we are led inexorably to the psychohistory of the era. What Sheridan doubly depicts is a national mirror-stage. It was precisely the archetypal father-figure who, whether he was aware of it or not, tried to own the desires of the young while demanding their sacrifice.

Although Tadhg would like to win his father's respect, when it comes to a fist-fight (Plate 11) he cannot beat the Yank. The Bull stands by the waterfall, the shamed and disappointed patriarch. When Tadhg can no longer get up, the Bull grabs both Tadhg and the Yank, brutally banging their heads together. Remarking on Harris' extraordinary 'level of passion' in *The Field*, Sheridan maintained that Harris was 'the key to the film': 'this is about evil and madness. Harris *was* crazy. In that scene where he killed the American, he *was* mad.' He adds that the cast had to grapple with 'some profound spiritual issues' and became 'kind of obsessed out there'.[80]

The waterfall scene in the film provides a glimpse of what the Bull must have been like with his two sons in the never-never time before the movie begins. At some level, however muted by affection, the father is obsessively out of control and controlling, deriding and belittling his children. The Bull assumes this admonitory role even towards the Yank, whom he blames for his family having left Ireland

Plate 11. At the waterfall.

during the bad times. As he kills the American the Bull insanely shouts, 'You tried to shame me. In front of my village. In front of my son. In front of God himself. Well, you'll not shame me, you'll not shame me, shame me, shame me, shame me, shame me, shame me.' This inspired speech, which draws together Séimí and the Bull's sense of shame, is not present in the 1989 screenplay and may well have been part of the borderline madness improvised by Harris during filming. In any event, in Sheridan's film, the Bull has gone mad, and by the following morning he is unable to distinguish between life and death, past and present, the Yank and his lost son. Folklorists often classify ancient Ireland as a 'shame culture': that is, a society in which being publicly humiliated is the worst imaginable fate. The Bull does everything in his power to avoid the shame of losing the field, only to discover himself endlessly entangled in escalating wrongdoing.

After killing the Yank and in response to Tadhg's announcement that he is leaving home, the Bull falls into a destructive rage. His wife speaks to him for the first time in eighteen years. Notably, she echoes *Mobile Homes* when she holds out a small mirror and forces him to look at himself (Plate 12). The Bull peers into it, searching in the recesses for himself or for Séimí: 'Are ye in there, Bull? Are ye in there, Séimí?' With or without the benefit of Lacanian psychoanalytic theory, we can see that the mirror is the zone of the Bull's unresolved psychic conflicts. In this scene, the Bull looks directly at the cinema audience, and we instantly become complicit in the explosive acting out of his mania. His mother's death, left unsanctified so that he and his father could bring in the hay, merges with the deaths of Séimí and the Yank as well as with the Bull's own loss of social identity.

All along, the Bull has been in denial over death, whether Séimí's or his mother's or the American's. He views the field's continuation in his family as recompense for these lives and a charm against future loss. It is therefore inevitable that he will create precisely what he fears most – the collapse of his family line. The field, his substitute for both sex and filiality, must be abandoned; we know the outcome from the

Plate 12. The Bull's mirror phase.

moment that the Bull tells Tadhg, 'This is what we'd be without the
land, boy', and blows a dry dandelion into the air (Plate 13).

Women and Intertextuality

Speaking in 1990, in the context of how *My Left Foot* had opened the
way for Irish filmmakers, Sheridan said, 'If Irish writers, especially,
got to know the medium, they could contribute a huge knowledge of
story and myth to films.'[81] Sheridan, responding to his times,
embroidered the lean structure of Keane's play with some hefty social
issues and themes. In addition, he layered the film with literary
allusions, accumulating them in the apocalyptic finale. Perhaps it was
the very spareness of the play – and the distance of its rural setting
from Sheridan's own inner-city life experiences – that impelled the

director to interweave *The Field* with references to classical Irish literature. Certainly the mythic strivings of the film suggest specific aesthetic precursors. The intertextual strands that Sheridan added to the play as a whole and that he lavished on the film's ending – particularly his references to W. B. Yeats's *On Baile's Strand* (1904) – significantly altered the structure and nature of Keane's work.

In addition to *On Baile's Strand*, Sheridan touches base with *Suibhne Astray*, *Purgatory* and the Irish mythic underpinnings to *King Lear*. Sheridan presents high points from the Irish literary heritage as a series of powerful scenes within a larger narrative of identity crisis. This strategy is itself a profound statement about cultural life in Ireland during the 1980s. Sheridan seems to be celebrating the fact that the intelligentsia of his era have used the literary heritage to work through the pressing contemporary problems of indigenous society. In this view, Ireland stands at a boundary between a tormented but

Plate 13. Object lesson.

eloquent past and an uncertain but irresistible future. In place of Keane's final scene, in which the Bull vigorously defends his actions against priest and sergeant, Sheridan introduces the sometimes awkward and extravagantly embellished narrative of Tadhg's decision to leave the land, the villagers' decanting the Yank from the lake, Mrs McCabe's abrupt return to communicating with her husband, the Bull's decline into an emotional no man's land and his driving both cattle and Tadhg into the sea.

These events are developed in terms of a cumulative intertextuality that risks sidelining the dominant story of traditional practices under siege from social change. However, the literary and cinematic allusions lacing the film's finale may be viewed as a way of reflexively indicating the use of allusion in aesthetic constructions. Intertextuality can thus be read as a key practice in producing cultural cohesion during the era of *The Crane Bag*. According to the semiotic theories fashionable at the time – especially those of Mikhail Bakhtin and Umberto Eco – any given narrative is composed from many prior discourses, and within a single film one can detect storied images from many precursors. Both author and text engage in the infinite play of sign systems.

One major influence on *The Field* was the film *Jean de Florette* (Plate 14). Indeed, Sheridan's film was briefly known around Dublin as 'Sean de Florette'. Released in 1986, Claude Berri's story of peasant land-hunger in rural France, continued in *Manon des Sources* (1986), received the British Academy's award for Best Film of 1987. César Soubeyran (Yves Montand) encourages his only surviving relative, Ugolin (Daniel Auteuil), in a plot to coerce a city man and his family to sell their land, on which a vital agricultural water source is located. Like *The Field*, *Jean de Florette* pairs a physically attractive but greedy patriarch with a less intelligent and less committed younger man as the adversaries to the city-bred outsider, Jean (Gérard Depardieu), who opposes their interests.

Unlike Bull McCabe and Tadhg, the Soubeyran males do not actively need the coveted land. The zone of possible influence between

Plate 14. Jean de Florette: *the interloper.*

the films is more subtle. We are asked to connect the Bull's memorable gesture of stretching out his arms, Christlike, to ward off Tadhg's fall from the cliff to Soubeyran's priestly blessing of his nephew with water from the hidden spring. We are asked to recognize that, in contrast to the play, Bull is seen switching his roof from thatch to slate not only because a slate-roofed cottage would enhance Tadhg's attractions for a potential bride's family but also because Sheridan must have admired the cinematography when Ugolin partially destroys the roof tiles on the home inherited by the urban Jean.

Additionally, we are asked to think about the death of the male while pondering the consequences of the survival of the female, a theme that *Manon des Sources* develops, if you will, on behalf of *The Field*, whose catastrophic ending seems to preclude a sequel. Manon (Emmanuelle Béart) is the wild and gorgeous woman with whom Ugolin eventually falls in love, creating an echo in the flashy figure of the tinker's daughter who wins Tadhg's loyalty. And all of the differences in detail and emotion attendant on the distance between

French and Irish rural life do not mask the films' parallel positions in the history of modernization. In both, there is only one local field that is worth its weight in gold, and there is only one source of invaluable water – obvious icons of local tradition. In both films, women come on the scene to fill the vacuum left by a bankrupt patriachy.

As always, Sheridan's depiction of women mixes misogyny with acceptance. In this duality, he is much influenced by Ireland's best-known poet. It has been said that no one writing in Ireland after the era of Yeats has entirely escaped his linguistic dominance: a Yeatsian idiom is one of the fundamental defaults in Irish discourse. In fleshing out the skeleton of Keane's play, Sheridan drew heavily on Yeats as a source of traditional tropes and gestures. Although this directorial decision has generated some degree of critical dismay, it must be granted that, given the Yeatsian influence, it is appropriate that Sheridan moved Keane's 1965 setting back to 1939, the year of the poet's death. In the film, references to Yeats's plays capture the flavour of Keane's struggle with the Abbey Theatre and Sheridan's own efforts at the Project Arts Centre to demystify the Abbey style. The situated history of dramatic production in Dublin engenders this cinematic story of a parent disowning and feeling shamed by its offspring. And the movie revisits that confrontation through cultural materials that Yeats, in his own way fighting the theatrical tide of his times, appropriated for his work – the Cuchulainn mythos and the pagan power associated with women.

Most commentators agree that the principal intertextual allusion in *The Field* is to Yeats's play, *On Baile's Strand*. In this play, Conchubar the king struggles to control his warrior Cuchulainn, to 'make him biddable as a housedog and keep him always at his hand'. In the play, part of the Cuchulainn story is told by the Fool to the Blind Man. Blind Man and Fool – Yeats's archetypes for the common people – discuss the fact that Aoife's son has come to kill Aoife's former lover, his father Cuchulainn. We realize that Cuchulainn will be unwittingly forced to kill his own son. We see that this staged conflict of father and son underwrites the similar battle of wills between Cuchulainn and Conchubar, the heroic past and the administered present. Aoife's challenge to the men of Ulster summons their fear of women and their knowledge that a woman's will cannot be 'oath-bound', as can a man's spirit. Like the tinker's daughter, Aoife threatens the safety of the increasingly domesticated men of Ulster.

Sheridan's implied view of women is entirely congruent with Yeats's presentation of Aoife in *On Baile's Strand*. The script tends to describe women in supernatural terms, labelling them witches and hypersexualizing them as part of the strongly gothic idiom that characterizes the screenplay. It is in a spirit of revenge that Aoife sends her son to fight his father. As the play's aura suggests, her agency cannot be distinguished from that of The Sidhe. Aoife's agency is continuous with this world of fairy and fate, which seeks to waylay and outwit offending mortals. The struggle between father and son has its origins in female rage.

Not knowing that he is a father, Cuchulainn claims to be happy not to have heirs. But Conchubar rejects Cuchulainn's assertion in terms that echo the Bull's familism:

> That is not true,
> For all your boasting of the truth between us;
> For there is no man having house and lands,
> That have been in the one family, called
> By that one family's name for centuries,
> But is made miserable if he know
> They are to pass into a stranger's keeping,
> As yours will pass.

Defending his view, Cuchulainn chides the lesser kings who unanimously enjoin him to take the High King's oath to guard the coastline: 'I understand it all. / It's you that have changed. You've wives and children now, / And for that reason cannot follow one / That lives like a bird's flight from tree to tree'.[82]

Cuchulainn, swearing allegiance to his king, nevertheless reminds the gathering that he still values 'Whatever life could make the pulse run quickly'. Although he has more in common with the chorus of Women who sing about change, Cuchulainn eventually pledges obedience. Then the wisdom of age grapples with the courage of youth; both Conchubar and Cuchulainn try to dissuade Aoife's champion from the duel. Ultimately, Cuchulainn discovers the magnitude of what he has done in killing the boy. Everything in the play, all of its ponderous ritual, reinforces the belief that this event was driven by supernatural forces.[83] But Cuchulainn, angry with Conchubar for binding his will, rushes out to kill the king. Instead of attacking the monarch, he attacks the sea. In *The Táin Bó Cuailnge*, the story of Cuchulainn is deeply interwoven with a story of cattle. Although in *The Táin* the Brown Bull defeats Ailill's White-horned Bull, it is a notable irony that the Brown Bull, like Sheridan's protagonist and like Cuchulainn, goes mad. In Yeats's version, it is the Fool who announces that a 'big wave' has 'mastered' the now-deranged Cuchulainn.[84] Either way, it is Cuchulainn's story that supplies Sheridan with the film's big finish.

Sheridan's screenplay includes an unfilmed sequence in which Mrs McCabe throttles a chicken, which Tadhg anonymously gives to the travelling woman who has caught his eye. Soon after Tadhg leaves his offering, the Bird steals the fowl for himself. This odd accretion to Keane's story, one which emphasizes the omnipresence of the Bird and his strategic use of everyone else's actions, seems to have its origin in *On Baile's Strand*. In the play, while the ultimate battle rages offstage, the Fool and the Blind Man grapple over the fate not of society but of a roasted chicken. In that the Blind Man and the Fool are aspects of the warrior and his king, the dramatic structure not only underlies the Bull–Bird relationship but also carries forward the demonstration that all aspects of male energy must yield to the power of the everyday.

In his classic study of Yeats, Harold Bloom speaks of the mixture of power and 'imaginative incoherence' that marks *On Baile's Strand*.[85]

To be sure, the play juggles a lot of themes that do not always neatly parse. Historical type and archetype, present and future, male and female, upper class and *hoi polloi*, natural and supernatural, the everyday and the extraordinary, tragically clash without the possibility of resolution in this drama. In Sheridan's hands, Yeatsian dramatis personae shape-shift into the Bull, the Bird, the Widow, the Yank, and everyone of note in Sheridan's film. And it is their inevitable disarray – part of the unavoidable messiness of social change – that Sheridan imports from the Yeatsian *oeuvre*. This strategy does not nullify the historical and ethnographic thrust of the play but rather creates a further dimension of meaning-construction out of the fundamental wellspring of social practices.

Fintan O'Toole has viewed Sheridan's accomplishment in *The Field* as containing and responding to the history of Irish drama. He calls *The Field* 'an extraordinary amalgam of Irish theatre from the Abbey of the early years of this century to the Project Arts Centre of the late 1970s, a kind of distillation of 80 years of images'.[86] As I see it, this gathering of images occurs mostly at the close of the film, and the cinematic ending is less a chronologically organized system of allusions than it is an intuitive, associative descant on literary themes. As the Bull mentally collapses, as the cattle plummet towards the sea, as Tadhg is carried over the cliff, the film undergoes a Yeatsian dreaming-back. The virtual dreamer is Irish culture, and the images that unravel before us are stock images from the cultural tradition. We get glimpses of Suibhne flying away in his anticlerical madness, of the Old Man in *Purgatory* killing his child, of Cuchulainn cradling the body of his dead son. Introducing these allusions as the finale dramatically underscores the undoing of tradition. As if Ireland were a stereotypical protagonist seeing his life flash before his eyes as he dies, so Sheridan's film arrays moments from literary history in the flurry of activity surrounding the emotional expiration of the Bull and his lifestyle. Each classic story is an intertext in the series of linked depictions that culminates in the film of *The Field*, itself structured

Plate 15. The Bird, the tinker's daughter and Mrs McCabe on the clifftop.

according to the 1980s obsession with intertextuality as a key to the construction of meaning.[87]

As a result of this allusive fanfare, the film concludes under the rubric of 'woman' and indicates an emergent social era no less contradictory than its precursor. After the dreaming-back, it is Mrs McCabe and the tinker's daughter who remain to survey the wreckage of the patriarchal order (Plate 15). Looking down from the clifftop on the Bull and Tadhg, the mother attests to the abandonment of masculinist–traditionalist Ireland. Reciting the Lord's Prayer, she is witness to the displacement of pre-Christian Ireland. Far from being associated entirely with a nostalgic primitivism, the two women lean more towards a forward-looking humanism barely emergent from the social wreckage. The monumental past has been explosively exorcised. At the same time, the long-term silence of the Bull's wife and the abject social status of the tinker's daughter are disavowed by this conclusion. The story never entirely renounces misogyny, but there is an effort to honour the survival of the female characters, and to sever the connection between shame and femaleness which the Bull has projected onto the women of his world.

Like Cuchulainn and other men in Celtic lore, the Bull has not maintained any but the most necessary ties with women. But, however silent or marginalized within the film's notional world of intact tradition, it is the women who speak and endure into the uncertain future. Keane's play ends in masculine stalemate, with the Bull holding his own against an unpacified authority, but the final scene of the film finds the women presiding over the chaos wrought by the Bird's tangling and the Bull's dreamlike, mythic madness. The erosion of familism involves not only loss but also possibility.

The final scene coexists uneasily with the fine-grained specificity that the movie retains from Keane's play and systematically enhances in its depiction of rural practices. Both play and film dramatically reimagine the 1958 Reamore murder in terms that directly speak to the weaving of the habitus from the embodied activities of human beings in a discrete rural environment. Sheridan's need to fill out his imagined world with literary and psychomythic elements finally attests to the modern inability to take the social system and its endless, unchanging reproduction for granted. As modernization progressed between mid century and the millennium, the effort to convey what intuitive confidence in social stability might have been like becomes more forced. The images available for portraying social practices feel less and less authentic, more pre-absorbed into cliché. Sheridan's film of *The Field* can easily be taken to task for its postcard views of Ireland, but in many ways the film uses those images to express anxiety about defining and maintaining Irishness in the face of modernization.

In mapping the path that leads from John B. Keane's play to Jim Sheridan's film, we have seen how the play and the film can serve to bring into focus not only leading concerns in Irish political and cultural debates but also much of what was taken for granted in each time period about the nature of Irish life, including its folkways, economy and self-understanding. Taken-for-granted ways of doing things enter into the play and the film not only as an implicit source of background information but also to compose the very fabric of both these texts. In the relatively settled world that Keane depicts, the Bull's personal crisis anticipates a breakdown of rural life that had only begun to make itself felt. Sheridan's Carraigthomond is set twenty years earlier than Keane's, but the issues it depicts are those of the 1980s, not the late 1950s and early 1960s. Partly because Sheridan used a romantically idealized vision of 1930s rural Ireland as a basis for an argument about the state of Ireland in the 1980s, the represented collapse of traditional practices is far more extreme than anything suggested by Keane's play. Keane gives us a Bull and a Bird who maintain their grip on the old ways, even if it is at an unexpectedly high price. Although Sheridan's protagonists start off by conforming to Keane's realist conventions, they become so overwhelmed by events, and so unable to go on in the old way, that only the most extravagant array of cultural tropes can serve to fill the abyss that has opened up within the social world. That said, in their own time these allegorical and intertextual elements emerged out of the texture of lived experience and remain, like the several versions of *The Field*, a testimony to the often unrecognized power of social practices.

CREDITS

Title:	The Field
Director:	Jim Sheridan
Release Year:	1990
Production Year:	1989
Production Company:	Granada Film Productions
	Sovereign Pictures
Country:	Great Britain
	Ireland

Cast:

Richard Harris	'Bull' McCabe
John Hurt	'Bird' O'Donnell
Tom Berenger	The American
Sean Bean	Tadgh McCabe
Frances Tomelty	Widow
Brenda Fricker	Maggie McCabe
Jenny Conroy	Tinker girl
Sean McGinley	Priest

Credits:

Jim Sheridan	Director
Steve Morrison	Executive Producer
Noel Pearson	Producer
Mary Alleguen	Production Manager
Grania O'Shannon	Location Manager
Don Geraghty	Location Manager
Arthur Lappin	Line Producer
James Davis	2nd Unit Director
Terry Needham	Assistant Director
Kevan Barker	Assistant Director
Seamus Collins	Assistant Director
David Byrne	Assistant Director
Nick McCarthy	Assistant Director
Jim Sheridan	Script
John B. Keane	Play by
Jack Conroy	Photography
Nuala Moiselle	Casting
Des Whelan	Camera Operator

David Worley	2nd Unit Camera Operator
James Davis	2nd Unit Photographer
Peter Dorney	Underwater Photographer
J. Patrick Duffner	Editor
Franck Conway	Production Designer
Maurice Foley	Special Effects Co-ordinator
Gerry Johnson	2nd Unit Special Effects
Josie MacAvin	Set Decorator
Joan Bergin	Costume Design
Janet O'Leary	Wardrobe
Tommie Manderson	Make-up Artist (Chief)
Ken Jennings	Make-up Artist
Peter Govey	Title/Opticals
Elmer Bernstein	Music
Irish Film Orchestras	Music performed by
Kathy Durning	Music Editor
Charlie O'Neill	Title Design
Nye Heron	Story Consultant
Ron Davis	Supervising Sound Editor
Tony Message	Dialogue Sound Editor
Kieran Horgan	Sound Recording
Brian Masterton	Sound Recording
Graham V. Hartstone	Sound Re-recording (Chief)
Nicholas Le Messurier	Sound Re-recording
Michael A. Carter	Sound Re-recording
Jenny Lee Wright	Foley Artist
Pauline Griffiths	Foley Artist
Bronco McLoughlin	Stunt Co-ordinator
Patrick Condren	Stunts
Harlan Cary Poe	Fight Co-ordinator
William Siddall	Dive Master
Cillian Gray	Diver
Running Time:	110
Colour Code:	Colour
Colour System:	Technicolor

Notes

1   Anthony Roche, *Contemporary Irish Drama: from Beckett to McGuinness* (New York: St Martin's Press, 1995), p. 7.

2   For texts of representative plays by Whitbread and Bourke, see Cheryl Herr, ed. *For the Land They Loved: Irish Political Melodramas 1890–1925* (Syracuse: Syracuse University Press, 1991).

3   John B. Keane, *Self-Portrait* (Cork: Mercier Press, 1964), p. 93.

4   Kathy Sheridan, 'John B. Good', *Irish Times* Weekend Section (21 July 2001), p. 1.

5   John B. Keane, *The Power of the Word* (Dingle: Brandon, 1989), p. 66.

6   Emer O'Kelly, 'John B Makes the Gradam', *Sunday Independent* (23 August 1998), p. L3.

7   Kathy Sheridan, p. 1.

8   Kathy Sheridan, p. 1.

9   Brinsley MacNamara, *The Valley of the Squinting Windows* (New York: Brentano's, 1919), p. 59.

10   Both Sheridan's screenplay and the film make use of the derogatory term 'tinker' as well as the designation 'traveller'. For that matter, Keane's play also speaks of tinkers.

11   John B. Keane, 'Kerry Nick-Names', in *Owl Sandwiches* (Dingle: Brandon, 1985), pp. 91–93.

12   John B. Keane, *The Field*, ed. Ben Barnes (Dublin: Mercier Press, 1991), p. 16. Further references will be noted parenthetically.

13   P. W. Joyce, *A Smaller Social History of Ancient Ireland* (Dublin: Longmans Green, 1908), p. 430.

14   Quoted from the RTÉ series *In Search of Ancient Ireland*, in Claire Callaghan, 'The Cow's the Thing in Ancient Ireland', *Irish Times* Weekend Section (16 June 2001), p. 8. The authoritative study of this topic is A. T. Lucas, *Cattle in Ancient Ireland* (Kilkenny: Boethius Press, 1989).

15   E. Estyn Evans, *The Personality of Ireland: Habitat, Heritage and History* (Dublin: Lilliput Press, 1992), pp. 38, 81.

16   Oliver MacDonagh, *States of Mind: a Study of Anglo-Irish Conflict 1780–1980* (London: Allen & Unwin, 1983), p. 34.

17   MacDonagh, p. 37.

18   MacDonagh, pp. 39, 41.

19   MacDonagh, p. 45.

20   MacDonagh, pp. 45, 48.

21   MacDonagh, p. 50.

22   Stage directions have been removed in this excerpt.

23   Keane, *The Field*, pp. 8–9.
24   Keane, *Durango: a Novel* (New York: Roberts Rinehart, 1995), p. 3.
25   Keane, *Durango*, p. 6.
26   Keane, *Durango*, p. 27.
27   Keane, *Durango*, p. 215.
28   Government of Northern Ireland, *The Marketing of Northern Ireland Agricultural Produce: a Report of Some Enquiries into the Conditions of Marketing Certain Classes of Agricultural Produce in Northern Ireland* (Belfast: HM Stationery Office, 1932), p. 77.
29   William Cotter Murray, *Michael Joe: a Novel of Irish Life* (1965; Dingle: Brandon, 1991), p. 221.
30   Murray, p. 223.
31   Joe Dowling, interview with author, 27 August 2001. Eamon Keane plays Dan Paddy Andy the matchmaker in Sheridan's film.
32   Keane, *Durango*, p. 3.
33   Sister Marie Hubert Kealey, *Kerry Playwright: Sense of Place in the Plays of John B. Keane* (London and Toronto: Associated University Presses, 1992), p. 20.
34   Anthony Roche, 'John B. Keane: Respectability at Last!', *Theatre Ireland*, Vol. 18 (April–June 1989), p. 30.
35   Quoted in Roche, 'John B. Keane', p. 30.
36   Conrad M. Arensberg, *The Irish Countryman: an Anthropological Study* (Garden City, NY: Natural History Press, 1968), p. 94.
37   Joseph J. Lee, *Ireland, 1912–1985: Politics and Society* (Cambridge: Cambridge University Press, 1989), p. 651.
38   Donna Birdwell-Pheasant, 'The Early Twentieth-Century Irish Stem Family: a Case Study from County Kerry', in *Approaching the Past: Historical Anthropology through Irish Case Studies*, eds. Marilyn Silverman and P. H. Gulliver (New York: Columbia University Press, 1992), p. 206.
39   Arensberg, p. 12.
40   Arensberg, pp. 67–68.
41   Pierre Bourdieu and Loïc J. D. Wacquant, *An Invitation to Reflexive Sociology* (Chicago: University of Chicago Press, 1992), p. 19.
42   Richard Jenkins, *Pierre Bourdieu* (London and New York: Routledge, 1992), p. 74.
43   Jenkins, pp. 74–75, 80.
44   Jenkins, pp. 89, 69, 71.
45   Bourdieu, *The Logic of Practice*, trans. Richard Nice (Cambridge: Cambridge UP), p. 14.
46   Nigel Floyd, '*The Field*', *Monthly Film Bulletin* (March 1991), p. 79.

47   Screenplay for *The Field*, p. 2. The screenplay is a 99-page typescript dated 15 and 20 September 1989. A copy of the screenplay was supplied by Ferndale Films for this project. I have indicated further quotations from the screenplay parenthetically.

48   Jim Sheridan, *Mobile Homes* (Dublin: Project Arts Centre, 1978), p. 73; Paddy Woodworth, 'Jim Sheridan: Singleminded in the Pursuit of His Ends', *Irish Times* (18 December 1993), p. 2.

49   Stephan Talty, 'Pluck of the Irish', *American Film*, Vol. 15 (September 1990), p. 34.

50   Jim Sheridan on 'Start the Week', BBC Radio 4, 1 February 1994.

51   Woodworth, p. 2.

52   Michael Dwyer, 'The Shooting of Gerry Conlon', *Irish Times* Weekend Section (8 May 1993), p. 1.

53   Michael Dwyer, 'The Power and the Glory of *The Field*', *Irish Times* (21 September 1990), p. 6.

54   Johnny Gogan, '*The Field*', *Film Base News* (November/December 1990), p. 19.

55   Derek Malcolm, 'Old Age Tension', *Guardian* (21 February 1991), p. 27.

56   Christopher Tookey, 'The Eloquence of Non-Communication', *Sunday Telegraph* Review Section (24 February 1991), p. 13.

57   Geoff Brown, review of *The Field*, *The Times* (21 February 1991), p. 21.

58   Nigel Floyd, p. 79.

59   Roger Ebert, '*The Field*', *Chicago Sun-Times* (1 March 1991), p. D9.

60   Rita Kempley, '*The Field*', *Washington Post* (25 January 1991), p. D7.

61   Peter Travers, 'Short Takes', *Rolling Stone* (10 January 1991), p. 53.

62   Kevin Rockett, 'Culture, Industry and Irish Cinema', in *Border Crossing: Film in Ireland, Britain and Europe*, eds. John Hill, Martin McLoone and Paul Hainsworth (Belfast: Institute of Irish Studies, 1994), p. 139.

63   Rockett, p. 138.

64   Rockett, p. 132.

65   Noel Pearson, interview with author, September 2001.

66   Talty, p. 37.

67   Michael D. Higgins, 'Liam O'Flaherty and Peadar O'Donnell: Images of Rural Community', *The Crane Bag*, Vol. 9 (1985), p. 44.

68   Vincent Kenny, 'The Post-Colonial Personality', *The Crane Bag*, Vol. 9 (1985), pp. 70–78.

69   Frantz Fanon, *The Wretched of the Earth* (New York: Grove Weidenfeld, 1968).

70   My transcription.

71   In addition to noting the problem of anachronism, Luke Gibbons asserts that *Man of Aran* desocialized the conditions of labour. Gibbons questions all concerned with *Man of Aran* because in it 'the everyday grind of work and production is desocialised and transformed into a heroic struggle between humanity and nature' and because the film putatively devalues 'language and community'. See Gibbons, 'Romanticism, Realism and Irish Cinema', *Cinema and Ireland*, Kevin Rockett, Luke Gibbons and John Hill (Syracuse, NY: Syracuse UP, 1988), pp. 201, 202.

72   Keane, *Self-Portrait*, pp. 34–35.

73   John B. Keane, *Three Plays: Sive, The Field, Big Maggie*, ed. Ben Barnes (New York: Irish American Books, 1990); *Big Maggie*, II, iii, p. 223.

74   See Peter Sheridan, *44: Dublin Made Me* (New York: Viking, 1999).

75   Yvonne Nolan, 'The Secret Passion of Peter's Da' [Review of *Forty-Seven Roses: a Memoir* by Peter Sheridan], *Irish Times* Weekend Section (1 September 2001), p. 9.

76   Fintan O'Toole also notices this connection to *The Field* in 'Theatrical Past Shapes *The Field*', *Irish Times* (23 September 1990), p. 10.

77   Sheridan, *Mobile Homes*, pp. 50, 51.

78   Sheridan, *Mobile Homes*, p. 52.

79   Sheridan, *Mobile Homes*, p. 53. The punctuation of ellipses is Sheridan's.

80   Talty, p. 49.

81   Talty, p. 49.

82   W. B. Yeats, *On Baile's Strand* (1904), repr. *Eleven Plays of William Butler Yeats*, ed. A. Norman Jeffares (New York: Collier, 1964), pp. 26, 30.

83   Yeats, pp. 32, 42.

84   Yeats, p. 43.

85   Harold Bloom, *Yeats* (Oxford: Oxford University Press, 1970), p. 157.

86   O'Toole, p. 10.

87   The personal reason for Sheridan's introduction of these dramatic flourishes may be found in his own career as innovative playwright. For Sheridan, the Irish dramatic tradition is flexible and available, and he sees part of the Irish filmmaker's job as introducing this theatrical corpus to the world at large.

Bibliography

Arensberg, Conrad M. *The Irish Countryman: an Anthropological Study*. Garden City, New York: Natural History Press, 1968.

Birdwell-Pheasant, Donna. 'The Early Twentieth-Century Irish Stem Family: a Case Study from County Kerry'. *Approaching the Past: Historical Anthropology through Irish Case Studies*. Eds. Marilyn Silverman and P. H. Gulliver. New York: Columbia University Press, 1992. 205–235.

Bloom, Harold. *Yeats*. Oxford: Oxford University Press, 1970.

Bourdieu, Pierre. *The Logic of Practice*, trans. Richard Nice. Stanford: Stanford UP, 1990.

Bourdieu, Pierre, and Loïc J. D. Wacquant. *An Invitation to Reflexive Sociology*. Chicago: University of Chicago Press, 1992.

Brown, Geoff. [Review] *'The Field'*. *The Times* (21 February 1991): 21.

Callaghan, Claire. 'The Cow's the Thing in Ancient Ireland'. *Irish Times* Weekend section (16 June 2001): 8.

Dwyer, Michael. [Review] 'The Power and the Glory of *The Field'*. *Irish Times* (21 September 1990): 6.

——. 'The Shooting of Gerry Conlon'. *Irish Times* Weekend section (8 May 1993): 1.

Ebert, Roger. [Review] *'The Field'*. *Chicago Sun-Times* (1 March 1991): D9.

Evans, E. Estyn. *The Personality of Ireland: Habitat, Heritage and History*. Dublin: Lilliput Press, 1992.

Fanon, Frantz. *The Wretched of the Earth*. New York: Grove Weidenfeld, 1968.

Floyd, Nigel. [Review] *'The Field'*. *Monthly Film Bulletin* (March 1991): 78–79.

Gibbons, Luke. 'Romanticism, Realism and Irish Cinema'. *Cinema and Ireland*. Kevin Rockett, Luke Gibbons and John Hill. Syracuse, NY: Syracuse UP, 1988. 194–257.

Gogan, Johnny. [Review] *'The Field'*. *Film Base News* (November/December 1990): 19.

Government of Northern Ireland. *The Marketing of Northern Ireland Agricultural Produce: a Report of Some Enquiries into the Conditions of Marketing Certain Classes of Agricultural Produce in Northern Ireland*. Belfast: HM Stationery Office, 1932.

Herr, Cheryl. Ed. *For the Land They Loved: Irish Political Melodramas 1890–1925*. Syracuse: Syracuse UP, 1991.

Higgins, Michael D. 'Liam O'Flaherty and Peadar O'Donnell: Images of Rural Community'. *The Crane Bag*, Vol. 9 (1985): 41–48.

Jenkins, Richard. *Pierre Bourdieu*. London and New York: Routledge, 1992.

Joyce, P. W. *A Smaller Social History of Ancient Ireland*. Dublin: Longmans Green, 1908.

Kealey, Sister Marie Hubert. *Kerry Playwright: Sense of Place in the Plays of John B. Keane*. London and Toronto: Associated University Presses, 1992.

Keane, John B. *The Bodhrán Makers*. Dingle: Brandon, 1986.

——. *Durango: a Novel*. New York: Roberts Rinehart, 1995.

——. *The Field*, ed. Ben Barnes. Dublin: Mercier Press, 1991.

——. *Owl Sandwiches*. Dingle: Brandon, 1985.

——. *The Power of the Word*. Dingle: Brandon, 1989.

——. *Self-Portrait*. Cork: Mercier Press, 1964.

——. *Three Plays: Sive, The Field, Big Maggie*. Ed. Ben Barnes. New York: Irish American Books, 1990.

Kempley, Rita. [Review] '*The Field*'. *Washington Post* (25 January 1991): D7.

Kenny, Vincent. 'The Post-Colonial Personality'. *The Crane Bag*, Vol. 9 (1985): 70–78.

Lee, Joseph J. *Ireland 1912–1985: Politics and Society*. Cambridge: Cambridge University Press, 1989.

Lucas, A. T. *Cattle in Ancient Ireland*. Kilkenny: Boethius Press, 1989.

MacDonagh, Oliver. *States of Mind: a Study of Anglo-Irish Conflict 1780–1980*. London: Allen & Unwin, 1983.

MacNamara, Brinsley. *The Valley of the Squinting Windows*. New York: Brentano's, 1919.

Malcolm, Derek. [Review] 'Old Age Tension'. *Guardian* (21 February 1991): 27–28.

Murray, William Cotter. *Michael Joe: a Novel of Irish Life*. 1965; Dingle: Brandon, 1991.

Nolan, Yvonne. 'The Secret Passion of Peter's Da'. *Irish Times* Weekend section (1 September 2001): 9.

O'Kelly, Emer. 'John B Makes the Gradam'. *Sunday Independent* (23 August 199): L3.

O'Toole, Fintan. 'Theatrical Past Shapes *The Field*'. *Irish Times* (23 September 1990): 10.

Roche, Anthony. *Contemporary Irish Drama: from Beckett to McGuinness*. New York: St Martin's Press, 1995.

Roche, Anthony. 'John B. Keane: Respectability at Last!'. *Theatre Ireland*, Vol. 18 (April–June 1989): 29–32.

Rockett, Kevin, Luke Gibbons and John Hill. *Cinema and Ireland*. Syracuse, NY: Syracuse UP, 1988.

Rockett, Kevin. 'Culture, Industry and Irish Cinema'. *Border Crossing: Film in Ireland, Britain and Europe*. Eds. John Hill, Martin McLoone and Paul Hainsworth. Belfast: Institute of Irish Studies, 1994. 126–139.

Sheridan, Jim, and Shane Connaughtan. *The Field*. Unpublished screenplay (15–20 September, 1989). Dublin: Ferndale Films.

Sheridan, Jim. *Mobile Homes*. Dublin: Project Arts Centre, 1978.

Sheridan, Kathy. 'John B. Good'. *Irish Times* Weekend section (21 July 2001): 1.

Sheridan, Peter. *44: Dublin Made Me*. New York: Viking, 1999.

Smith, Gus, and Des Hickey. *John B: the Real Keane*. Cork and Dublin: Mercier Press, 1992.

Talty, Stephan. 'Pluck of the Irish'. *American Film*, Vol. 15 (September 1990): 33–37, 49.

Tookey, Christopher. [Review] 'The Eloquence of Non-Communication'. *Sunday Telegraph* Review section (24 February 1991): 13.

Travers, Peter. [Review] 'Short Takes'. *Rolling Stone* (10 January 1991): 53.

Woodworth, Paddy. 'Jim Sheridan: Singleminded in the Pursuit of His Ends'. *Irish Times* (18 December 1993): 2.

Yeats, W. B. *On Baile's Strand* (1904). Repr. *Eleven Plays of William Butler Yeats*. Ed. A. Norman Jeffares. New York: Collier, 1964.

Ollscoil na hÉireann, Gaillimh